Psychological Perspectives of Education

Psychological Perspectives of Education
(Elementary Level)

B.K. Pal
Neera Sadh

SP SHIPRA
SHIPRA

Rs. 195, US$ 8

ISBN: 978-93-86262-06-6

2023 3rd Impression
(2019, First Published 2017)

Psychological Perspectives of Education: Elementary Level

Published by:
SHIPRA PUBLICATIONS
LG 18-19, Pankaj Central Market,
I.P. Ext., Patparganj, Delhi 110092, India
+91 11 22235152/ 6152, 96500 28065
info@shiprapublication.com
www.shiprapublication.com

Preface

The Psychology of Learning is theoretical and practical science. Learning is a process that depends on experiences that lead to long term changes in behaviural potential. Main assumption behind all learning psychology is that the effects of the environment, reinforcement, conditioning etc. provide psychologists with the best information from which to understand human behaviour. According to Charles E. Skinner "Educational psychology deals with the behaviour of human beings in educational situations." Thus educational psychology is a behavioural science with two main references: "human behaviour and education". E. A. Peel says "Educational psychology is the science of education; it helps the teacher to understand the development of his pupil, range and limits of their capacities, the processes by which they learn their social responsibilities."

This book, *Psychological Perspectives of Education* (*Elementary Level*) is based upon the new curriculum prescribed by the State Council of Educational Research and Training New Delhi for the trainees of Diploma in Elementary Education. All the efforts have been made to make content relevant, precise, sufficient and orderly mannered. The language used is easy, simple and understandable. The units contain relevant contents with proper heading, sub-headings along with concerned figures and Educational implications of the topics. This book is also helpful for C.T.E.T. preparation, B.Ed., B.T.C. and D.El.Ed. trainees of various Universities, DIETs and SCERT/State Institute of Education of different states.

We thank all the authors and publishers whose works have been used in enhancing the value of this book for the readers. We express the gratitude to Shipra Publications for helping us to bring this book into limelight.

B.K. Pal
Neera Sadh

Contents

Contents

1
Understanding Learning

At the time of birth each individual is born with some innate tendencies, but these tendencies are not enough in the struggle for life. For the existence of life, human comes in contact with environment and starts reacting. In this process of interaction the individual acquires some new knowledge, skills and attitude. It also results in changes or modification in his/her behaviour. In this way, the behaviour of an individual is changed or modified through direct and indirect experiences. This change in behaviour brought about by experiences or training are generally known as learning. Thus learning is a relatively permanent change in the behaviour or response and is an enrichment of experience.

1.0 DEFINITIONS

Psychologists have given various definitions of learning:

Crow and Crow: "Learning is the acquisition of habits, knowledge and attitudes. It involves new ways of doing things and it operates on an individual's attempts to overcome obstacles or to adjust to new situation. It represents progressive changes in behaviour".

Woodworth: "Learning is a process of acquiring new knowledge and new responses".

Hilgard defined learning as "a change in subject's behaviour to a given situation brought about by his repeated experiences in that situation, provided that the behavioural change cannot be explained on the basis of native response tendencies, maturation or temporary states of the subject (e.g., effect of fatigue, drugs, etc.)."

In the light of above definitions it can be concluded that learning is a process in which necessary changes in the behaviour of an individual takes place through direct & indirect experience. It is also clear from the definition of Hilgard that these changes in behaviour do not include changes due to maturation, illness, effect of fatigue and use of intoxicants.

Therefore, learning is a process of bringing change in behaviour (relatively permanent) due to experience and training.

1.1 NATURE OF LEARNING

From the definitions and discussions the nature of learning can be discussed under these points:

1. Learning is a process not product.
2. It involves all those experiences and training of an individual (right from birth) which help him to produce change in behaviour.
3. Learning is purposeful and goal-oriented.
4. Learning is a relatively permanent change in behaviour. These changes do not include change in behaviour due to maturation, illness, effect of fatigue, drugs etc.
5. Learning is universal. It means every creature that lives learns.
6. Learning is a continuous and never ending process that extends from womb to tomb.
7. The scope of learning is too wide. It is a very comprehensive process, which covers all fields. These fields widely called 'domains' as: Cognitive domain, Affective domain, Psychomotor domain of human behaviour.
8. Learning prepares an individual for any adjustment and adoption that may be necessary.
9. Learning involves new ways of doing things but there is no limit to adopt these ways and means.
10. Learning involves reconstruction of experiences. It means what has been learnt by an individual previously always remains in the state of modification in light of new and richer experiences gained by that individual.
11. Learning is transferable from one situation to another, and from one person to another.
12. All types of learning is not directly observable.

1.2 THE PROCESS OF LEARNING

Learning is a process which has continuity. Regarding the process of learning Smith says that "learning process involves a motive or drive, an attractive goal and a block to the attainment of the goal. All these are essentials".

It is clear from the Smith's view that learning is carried over through various steps. The first step in the learning process is motive or need.

Motive is the force which compels the individual to act. It energises the behaviour of individuals in desirable direction. If there is motive or need, the person has to set definite goals. These goals attract him. It is second step of learning.

In the third step, the learner or individual faces some obstacles or barrier to attain the goal. If there is no barrier or difficulty in attaining the goal, then there is no need to learn new knowledge, skills or behaviour. Therefore, blocks or barrier are important part of learning as individual learn new things or modifies behaviour to overcome these obstacles and to attain the goal.

The process of learning can be presented diagrammatically as:

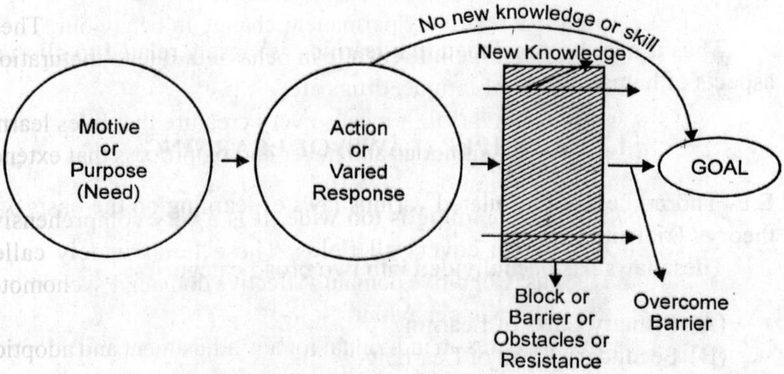

1.3 IMPORTANCE OF LEARNING

Learning plays an important part in human life. It is the basis of success in life. It determines the behaviour of an individual learning which is not limited to the classroom activities. It is a very comprehensive process and it covers all the aspects of human personality.

Importance of learning can be discussed unuer the following points:

Learning helps in bringing desirable changes in behaviour: It is a process that helps in bringing desirable changes in the behaviour of learner in all its three domains as cognitive, affective, psychomotor.

Learning helps in proper or adequate adjustment: The success in life is closely related to the individual's adjustment with own self and environment. Learning helps the person in making proper adjustment.

Learning helps in the achievement of teaching-learning objectives: Learning helps the learner to acquire new knowledge, skills, habits, attitude, interests, etc., and consequently the objectives of teaching-learning process can be effectively achieved.

Learning helps in proper growth and development of individual: Learning plays an important role in all the aspects of growth and development as physical, emotional, language, moral and social development.

Learning helps in the all-round development of personality: The main objectives of education is the all-round development of personality of the learner. To fulfil this objective, learning plays an important role as it influence all the aspects of personality.

Learning helps in achieving the goals of life: Every individual has some goals in life. To realise these goals he/she has to acquire/learn new knowledge, skills, attitude etc. also to modify behaviour to achieve the goal. Here learning plays an important part to achieve the goal.

Thus it may be concluded that learning is closely related to all the aspects of human life.

1.4 PRINCIPLE (LAWS) OF LEARNING

E.L. Thorndike has formulated various laws of learning on the basis of theory 'Trial and Error'.

These laws has been divided into two broad categories:

(A) Primary Laws of Learning
(B) Secondary Laws of Learning

These laws are further divided into various laws as:

(A) Primary Laws of Learning

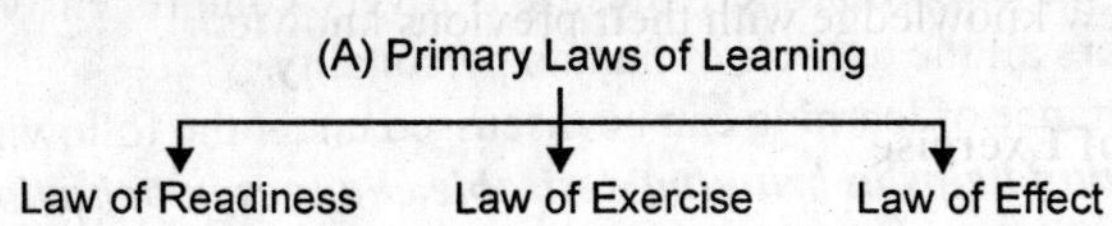

(B) Secondary Laws of Learning

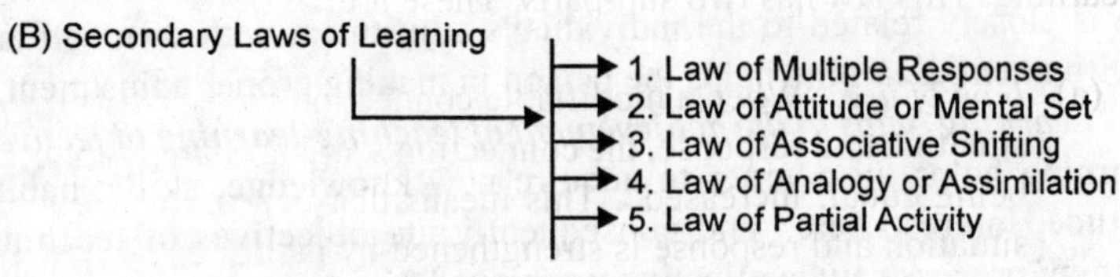

The description and classroom applications of the above laws are given as follows:

(A) PRIMARY LAWS OF LEARNING

Law of Readiness

Readiness means 'preparation for action'. Readiness is an essential part of learning. If the learner is ready to learn, he/she learns more quickly, effectively and with more satisfaction than when he/she is not ready to learn. The readiness should be mentally and physically both. If the learner is not physically and mentally ready, all the efforts of teaching-learning process would be useless. Readiness also depends upon the maturation and experiences of learner.

Educational Implications

1. Before teaching or organising any activity, children should be made ready to learn. For this purpose teacher should motivate students by tellings story related to the topic, asking questions related to their previous knowledge about the topic, organise relevant activities etc. This will arouse the attention and interest of the students.
2. While organising activities or asking questions or teaching new topics, the maturation level of students should be considered. Contents and activities should be according to the physical and mental level of students.
3. Teacher should arouse the interest of students by linking the new knowledge with their previous knowledge and daily life.

The Law of Exercise

This law is also known as 'Law of practice' or Law of repetition', which means that drill and practice helps in increasing efficiency and durability of learning. This law has two sub-parts. These are:

(a) *Law of use*. "When a modifiable connection is made between a situation and response, the connection's strength is, other things being equal, increased". This means that connection between situation and response is strengthened by practice".

(b) *Law of disuse*. "When a modifiable connection is not made between a situation and response, during a length of time, the connection's strength is decreased". It means when practice is discontinued, connections between situations and response become weak.

In brief, it can be said that law of exercise emphasises the need for practice, repetition or drill work in the process of learning. 'Practice makes a man perfect', is a well-known proverb which is associated with this law.

Educational Implications

(i) More and more opportunities should be provided to the students to use and repeat the experiences they get in the class so that learning can be long lasting.
(ii) Practice with various skills can be developed like music, painting, shorthand, dancing, cycling, etc.
(iii) Practice with handwriting of the students can be improved.
(iv) Correct pronunciation has to be learnt by practice.
(v) Various concepts of mathematics are closely related to practice, such as counting, tables, etc.
(vi) To maintain the connection for longer period, review or recapitulation of the learned material is necessary.
(vii) Teacher should provide opportunity for discussion of learnt material. This will help students for effective learning.

The Law of Effect

According to this law "when a modifiable connection between situation and response is made and is accompanied, followed by a satisfying state of affairs, the connections strength is increased, but when it is made and accompanied by an annoying state of affairs its strength is decreased".

It means that learning is effective when it is associated with satisfaction and pleasure, but when the learner is dissatisfied, learning progress is blocked.

This law emphasises on the role of reward and punishment in the process of learning. Reward motivates and encourage the learner, whereas punishment discourages him/her.

But later on Thorndike modified his earlier law of effect, as "satisfaction strengthens the bond but annoyance does not weaken it".

Educational Implications

(i) To make learning effective classroom experiences and other activities should be meaningful, satisfactory, pleasant and according to the mental level of the students.

(ii) The content and teaching-learning material should be designed and organised in such a way that learner should get satisfaction and take interest in it.

(iii) Teacher should be sympathetic and must enjoy teaching work.

(iv) Rewards and punishment should be applied properly to make learning effective.

(v) Individual differences should be taken into account while teaching.

1.5 SUBORDINATE/SECONDARY LAWS OF LEARNING

Apart from these three laws, Thorndike gave the following subordinate laws:

Law of Multiple Response

This law states that when an individual faces new situations, he/she tries many responses before attempting the right response.

Educational Implications

(i) The learner should be encouraged to do his/her work independently. He/she must try the various responses before arriving at a correct one. Here learners learns from their own error.

(ii) The teacher should provide help to the students. Also care should be taken that student may not waste time and energy by repeating the same mistake again and again.

Law of Set or Attitude

According to this law, the mental set and attitude of the learner plays an important role in learning. If learner has positive attitude towards learning then learning takes place easily and effectively.

Educational Implications

(i) Teacher should assist the students to develop positive attitude towards various activities (curricular & co-curricular).

(ii) To develop favourable attitude towards learning, the content and TLM used by the teacher should be meaningful and interesting and according to the level of the students.

(iii) Classroom environment should be congenial and teacher's personality should be integrated and balanced.

Law of Analogy and Assimilation

This principal states that when an individual is confronted with a new situation, he/she makes use of old experiences. The learner responds to the new situation as he/she did in the previous similar situation. For example, the learning of driving a motor cycle is facilitated by the earlier acquired skill of riding a bicycle.

Educational Implications

(i) The new knowledge should be linked with the previous knowledge and experience of the students.

(ii) Teacher should use the maxims of teaching like known to unknown while teaching. Child must, also be encouraged to see similarities and dissimilarities between the different kind of stimuli.

Law of Associative Shifting

According to this law response may be shifted from one situation to another which is presented at the same time. This law is related to law of transfer of learning.

Law of Pre-potency of Elements

This law states that the learner reacts to the learning situation in a selective manner. He selects the essential or selective elements in the situation and neglects the irrelevant elements. The ability to deal with the essential and relevant part of the situation makes analytical and insightful learning possible.

LEARNING THEORIES

The primary objective of instruction in school is to bring certain desirable changes in the behaviour of learner through the process of learning. To fulfil this objective, a teacher must have the knowledge of how a child learns the process?, operations and approaches to learning, principles and techniques of learning etc. Various psychologists have tried to perform experiments to explain the various aspects of learning and as a result various learning theories have been developed. These theories represent the nature, process, laws, methods and techniques of learning.

Various theories of learning may broadly be divided in two categories:

I. Connectionist or Behaviourist or Associative or Stimulus Responses (S-R) Theories

In these types of theories, the learning can be interpreted in terms of the change in the behaviour of learner brought about by association or connection of response to a series of stimuli. The various theories in this category are as follows:

(i) Classical conditioning theory by Pavlov
(ii) Watson's learning theory
(iii) Guthrie's learning theory
(iv) Trial & error theory by E.L. Thorndike
(v) Hull's theory of learning
(vi) Operant Conditioning theory by B.F. Skinner

In the above six theories, first three are S-R type theories without reinforcement and last three are S-R theories with reinforcement.

II. Cognitive Field Theories

These theories interpret learning as the change in the field consisting of learner and his environment and the learner's perception of field. In these theories, emphasis is given on the insight, purpose and understanding in the process of learning.

The following theories are included in this category:

(i) Gestalt or insight theory of learning by Kohler, Koffka, Max Wertheimer, Kurt Lewin.
(ii) Tolman's sign Gestalt theory of learning.

Here some important theories have been discussed in detail. These are:

(a) Trial and Error theory by E.L. Thorndike
(b) Classical Conditioning by I.P. Pavlov
(c) Operant Conditioning by B.F. Skinner
(d) Insight theory by Kohlar *et al.*

1.6 TRIAL AND ERROR THEORY OF LEARNING
Or
STIMULUS-RESPONSE (S-R) THEORY OF LEARNING
Or
BOND THEORY OF LEARNING
Or
THEORY OF CONNECTIONISM

Edward Lee Thorndike (1874-1949), an American Psychologist is the propagator of Trial and Error Theory of Learning. He conducted a series of experiments on learning with animals. On the basis of experiments he stated that connections are formed in the nervous system between stimuli and responses. These connections formed are represented by S-R symbol and can be described by another word 'bond'. Therefore, this theory is also known as "Bond Theory of Learning" or "Theory of Connectionism". On this, Thorndike has written, "Learning is connecting. The mind is man's connection system".

Fig. Thorndike's cat trying to come out

According to Thorndike, learning takes place by trial and error. When an individual faces a problem, he/she first tries one solution, if it does not work, he rejects it and tries another, and so on. But as the number of trials goes on increasing, the errors or irrelevant responses go on decreasing. Thus, in trial and error method, the learner makes random activities and finally reaches the goal accidently. Thorndike called it, "learning by selecting and connecting", as it provides an opportunity for the selection of proper or correct response and associates with it adequate stimuli.

Experiment Conducted by Thorndike

The Puzzle Box Experiment by Thorndike: Thorndike's classical experiments on cat in puzzle box are widely known and quoted in psychology of learning. In one such experiment, the hungry cat was put in the puzzle box. A fish was placed outside the box. The smell of fish worked as a strong motive for hungry cat. The box was designed in such a way that the door of the box could be opened by pressing a lever inside the box. At first, the cat made several random movements like jumping, scratching, walking around, dashing, shaking moveable parts, claws and bites at the bars to come out from the box. All efforts went in vain. At last, the cat's paw fell on the lever and the door opened by chance. The cat came out and ate the fish. In subsequent trials when the experiment was repeated the irrelevant movement made by the cat decreased and the time taken to come out from the box also decreased with every trial. After many trials, the cat was able to open the door (by directly striking the latch with paw) without any error and it actually learned the way to open the door.

The experiment sums up the various stages in the learning process through trial and error as:

(i) **Goal:** Goal plays very important role in learning process. Without goal all learnings are useless. In this experiment to get the food by getting out of the box was goal.

(ii) **Drive:** Drive compels the learner to act. The drive should be strong. In the present experiment it was hunger which was intensified by the sight and smell of fish.

(iii) **Block:** Block as barrier are essential to learn new things. Here, closed door of the box was the barrier for cat.

(iv) **Random movements:** Random movements are helpful to reach the goal. In the present experiment jumping, scratching, biting the bars, moving around by the cat were the random movements.

(v) **Chance success:** As a result of random movements, we get success by chance. In the experiment, after some random movements, the paw of the cat fell on the level and door opened by chance.

(vi) **Selection:** Random movements do not continue for long time as the learner selects the correct response after some trials. Here, gradually the cat recognised the correct method to open the door.

(vii) **Fixation:** It is a stage of errorless performance. Correct responses are fixed. In the experiment, the cat learned the proper way of opening the door without any error.

Based upon the experiment done by E.L. Thorndike, this theory can be summarised as follows:

- Learning involves trial and error or selection and connection.
- Learning is the result of formation of connections.

LAWS OF LEARNING

On the basis of experiments, Thorndike propounded the various laws of learning. For details refer to page numbers 5 to 9 (1.4 to 1.5).

1. Primary laws of learning
2. Secondary laws of learning

Educational Implications of Theory

Thorndike's Trial and Error Theory and his basic laws have enough educational significance. He tries to explain the learning process on the basis of systematically conducted series of experiments. Some important implications are as follows:

(i) *Importance of motivation:* Motivation and learning are closely related to each other. Motive is a force that compels an individual to act in a particular direction. Without motivation learning is impossible. Therefore, students must be properly motivated before they are taught. Teacher should have the knowledge of various motivational techniques.

(ii) *Importance of readiness:* Readiness means "preparation for action". Learner should be physically and mentally ready to learn.

Maturation and experiences of learner are related to readiness. If learner is ready to learn, he learns more quickly and effectively. To ready the students, teacher should test the interest, attitude, ability, aptitude, so that he/she can become aware about the capability of learner.

(iii) *Importance of exercise or repetition:* This theory states that in order to master a complex task, practice is must. For this purpose the teacher should provide opportunities to students to use and repeat the content or experience they get in class. Each task initially seems to be difficult and fatiguing but as practice continues, it becomes smoother and requires less effort.

(iv) *Importance of experiences:* This theory gives importance to previous experiences to learn new things. The teacher must link the new knowledge to the previous knowledge, experience and daily life of students.

(v) *Role of reward and punishment:* Both reward and punishment play a significant role in the process of learning. According to this theory learning takes place properly when it results in satisfaction, and learner derives pleasure out of it. Reward gives motivation and encouragement to the learner and punishment discourages him. Teacher should properly use the reward and punishment.

(vi) *Useful for learning of skills:* Various skills like dancing, painting, cycling, driving, music etc. are learnt by trial and error. We learn many of our activities of daily routine through trial and error.

(vii) *Useful for memorising:* Tables of mathematics, poetry/poems, formulaes can be learnt by practice.

(viii) *Individual differences:* According to this theory, individual differences should be considered during learning. Learner's interest, attitude, mental level, capabilities should be taken in to account. Also teacher should encourage the students to work independently so that he/she can try the various solutions to solve the problem by arriving at the correct one.

In short, Thorndike's theory have contributed a lot in the field of education. According to this theory learning is purposeful and goal oriented. It has given importance to repetition, practice, motivation, reward and punishment in the process of learning.

Limitations of Trial and Error Theory

This theory has been criticised by various psychologists on various grounds as follows:

(i) *Mechanical:* This theory is mechanical. It considers man as a machine. But human being has thinking and insight. They use their insight to do things. Mechanical repetition without understanding is useless.

(ii) *Wastage of time and energy on useless efforts:* In this theory there is wastage of time and energy due to useless efforts without understanding the situation.

(iii) *Emphasis on rote learning:* This theory ignores understanding, insight, thinking and gives more emphasis on rote learning. The effect of rote memory is momentary.

(iv) *Not much useful for bright students and higher classes:* This theory is useful for lower classes and backward students. Bright students and those of higher classes are not much benefited with this theory, as they use their insight, understanding and thinking in the process of learning.

1.7 CLASSICAL CONDITIONING

Russian psychologist Ivan P. Pavlov discovered the theory of classical conditioning. He was basically interested in studying the process of gastric secretion in dogs. He got Nobel Prize in 1904 on his research on digestive process. This theory is also known as:

- Theory of conditioned response
- Substitution of response theory
- S-type conditioning

Conditioned response means responding naturally to an unnatural situation or a unnatural stimulus. For example, when we feel hungry, the sight of food causes salivation in our mouth. This is our natural response. But it is common experience that the ringing of recess bell in schools generally leads secretion of saliva in the mouth of children. This is our conditional response. This response is reinforced when the recess bell is repeatedly followed by some meal, lunch or refreshment.

Pavlov conducted experiments on dogs to understand the process of classical conditioning in detail.

Pavlov's Experiment

In this experiment, a dog was kept hungry and tied to an experimental table which was controlled with some mechanically devices. A bell was rung and immediately thereafter food was served to the dog. This activity was repeated several times under similar conditions. A bell was rung at the time food was served to the dog, and saliva would secrete in the mouth of dog. After some days it was observed that even though only the bell was rung, and no food was served, but the dog still salivated to the sound of bell. This association between the bell and food resulted in acquisition of a new response by a dog i.e., 'Salivation at the sound of the bell'. This has been termed as classical conditioning.

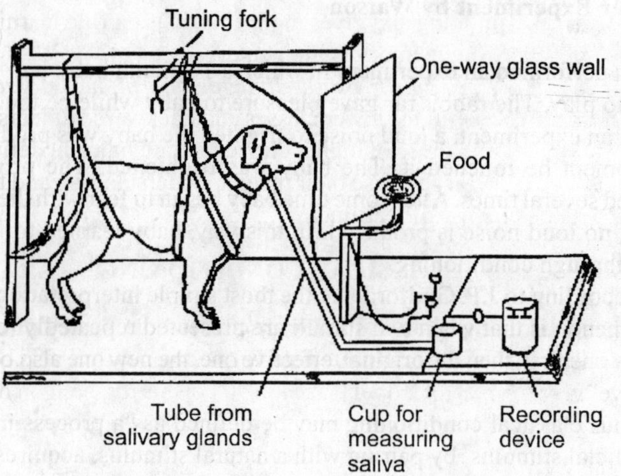

Fig.: Diagrammatic view of the experiment conducted by Pavlov (Garrett, General Psychology, p. 254)

Here,

- Food is an unconditioned stimulus or natural stimulus and termed as 'UCS'.
- Secretion of saliva for food is an unconditional response or natural response i.e. 'UCR'.
- Sound of bell is conditioned stimulus or artificial stimulus which is 'CS'.
- Secretion of saliva to sound of bell is conditioned response i.e. 'CR'.

The procedure of conditioned response can be presented as follows:

Stages of Conditioning	Nature of Stimulus	Nature of Response
I Stage (Before Conditioning)	Food → (UCS) →	Salivation (UCR)
II Stage (Under Conditioning)	Sound of the bell + food → (CS+UCS) →	Salivation (UCR)
III Stage (After Conditioning)	Sound of the bell → (CS) →	Salivation (CR)

Another Experiment by Watson

Watson performed an experiment in which a 11 month baby was given a rabbit to play. The rabbit fur gave pleasure to baby while he touched it. During an experiment, a loud noise to frighten the baby was produced at the moment he touched it. The baby was frightened. The process is repeated several times. After some time baby began to fear with the rabbit, even if no loud noise is produced. In this way, baby learned to fear the rabbit through conditioning.

According to J.P. Guilford, "...the most simple interpretation of this phenomenon is that when two stimuli are presented repeatedly together, the new one first, then the original, effective one, the new one also becomes effective".

Thus classical conditioning may be defined as "a process in which an artificial stimulus, by pairing with a natural stimulus, acquires all the characteristics of natural stimulus". In the above experiment, artificial stimulus (sound of bell) by pairing with natural stimulus (food), acquired the characteristics of food and succeeded in eliciting the response of salivation.

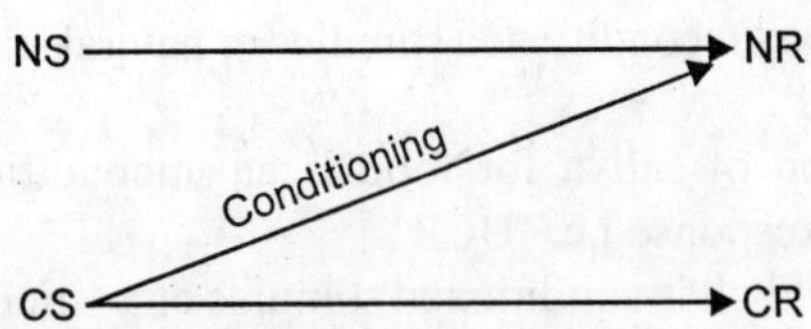

Classical conditioning is also known as substitution learning because an artificial stimulus is substituted in place of natural stimulus.

Principles of Conditioning

The success of conditioning depends upon the following principles:

(1) *Principle of Intensity:* Principle of intensity states that the conditioned stimulus (CS) should be of great intensity. More intense the CS, more rapidly and effectively conditioning will proceed.

(2) *Principle of Consistency:* It means that the process of conditioning should be repeated several times without any change, i.e. for strong and effective conditioning CS and UCS should be repeated a number of times.

(3) *Principle of Time:* Conditioning depends upon the optimal time interval between the presentation of the conditioned stimuli (CS) and unconditioning stimuli (UCS). Based on the time relation between CS and US, conditioning are basically four types:

 (a) *Simultaneous Conditioning.* When the CS and UCS are presented together then it is called simultaneous conditioning.

 (b) *Delayed Conditioning.* In delayed conditioning UCS follows the CS. It is reported that delayed conditioning is most effective way of acquiring CR.

 (c) *Trace Conditioning.* Here CS precedes the UCS but some time there is gap between the two. It is not effective.

 (d) *Backward Conditioning:* It is mostly unsuccessful. Here UCS is presented prior to CS.

(4) *Principle of Age:* The process of conditioning is valuable at all ages, especially in early childhood.

(5) *Principle of Stimulus Generalisation:* Generalisation is a process in which a conditioned response to a stimulus is generalised to similar category of stimuli. For example, if we are conditioned to one thing i.e. bell, then we would be conditioned more or less to all sorts of bells.

(6) *Principle of Extinction:* If the sound of bell, i.e. CS is not followed by food (UCS), then a stage comes when the dog stops to secrete saliva. This process is known as extinction.

(7) *Principle of Spontaneous Recovery:* When the dog is brought out of the experimental set up and the process of conditioning is repeated, after sometime the dog responds to conditioned stimulus (sound of bell) by secreting saliva. This process is called spontaneous recovery.

(8) *Principle of External Barriers:* It was observed that if there is any external barrier as noise or other distraction (which may draw the attention of dog) during the process of conditioning, then conditioning takes time. The occurrence of the external barrier blocks or inhibits the conditioned response.

Educational Implications of Classical Conditioning

Implications of classical conditioning may be discussed under these points:

(i) *Formation of good habits:* Habits like punctuality, cleanliness, obedience, respect for elders, discipline can be developed with the help of conditioning. In this reference Pavlov stated that "different kinds of habits based on training, education and discipline of any sort are nothing but a long chain of conditioned reflex."

(ii) *Elimination of fear and phobia:* Fear and phobia are aroused by unnatural, irrelevant or unusual stimuli. When things and objects are associated with unpleasant experiences and a sort of generalisation is made, phobia appears. Such fear and phobia can be removed by deconditioning or associating the objects and things that cause fear with pleasant stimuli.

(iii) *Helpful in language learning:* Conditioning can be used to teach the alphabets in any language. For example, to teach letter "A", it should be associated with apple or picture of apple. Thus, this theory also emphasises the use of teaching aids in teaching-learning process.

(iv) *Useful in developing positive attitude:* Positive attitude towards teachers, parents, subjects, school can be developed with help of conditioning. A teacher with non-psychological method of teaching and authoritative behaviour, may be disliked by the students. In the same way, some unpleasant experiences associated with school environment and subject may develop a negative attitude among children. Therefore, teachers, parents and school authority should create healthy environment and favourable situations in school and at home so that children may develop positive attitude.

(v) *Useful in adjustment:* Conditioning plays a very important role to make adjustment of individual with the environment. Healthy environment and favourable conditions should be associated with the children.

(vi) *Use of audio-visual aids:* This theory emphasises the use of audio-visual aids in teaching-learning process. For effective learning it is important that teacher should use audio-visual aids to teach any concept. For example, the teacher shows the picture of cow, along with the written word 'cow'; teacher speaks the word 'cow' just after showing the picture of 'cow' and asks the students to say cow every time when the picture is presented. After sometime students speaks the word 'cow' without showing the picture.

Along with some general contributions of classical conditioning are:

(vii) useful in mental hospitals.
(viii) useful in the treatment of delinquent, problematic and maladjusted children.
(ix) useful in training the animals.

1.8 OPERANT CONDITIONING

B.F. Skinner, an American Psychologist of Harvard University was the propagator of this theory. Operant conditioning is also known as instrumental conditioning and R-type conditioning. Skinner developed his own apparatus and method of observation to study and analyse behaviour. He recognised two types of behaviour that are produced in different experimental procedure:

(i) Respondent Behaviour
(ii) Operant Behaviour

Respondent Behaviour: Respondent behaviour is that behaviour or response which is caused or elicited by known stimuli or event in the environment. Respondent behaviour is associated with S-type conditioning as in case of Pavlovian conditioning. Respondent behaviour is internal and personal. Examples of respondent behaviour include all the reflexes as jerking one's own hand when jabbed with a pin, blinking of eye in the presence of flash light, etc.

Operant Behaviour: Operant behaviour is an emitted response which is not associated with any known stimulus. Skinner associates this behaviour with R-type conditioning.

He called his procedure/theory as R-type conditioning or operant conditioning. Operants are those behaviour/actions or responses or operations which are enacted by animals and human beings voluntarily and are under their control. The term operant is used because organism operates on the environment. This theory is also known as 'instrumental conditioning' as the activities, responses or actions of the organism become instrumental in attaining desired goal.

According to this theory: "Behaviour is learned, maintained and changed by its consequences".

Skinner conducted a series of experiments on rats and pigeons. One of such experiments is elaborated below:

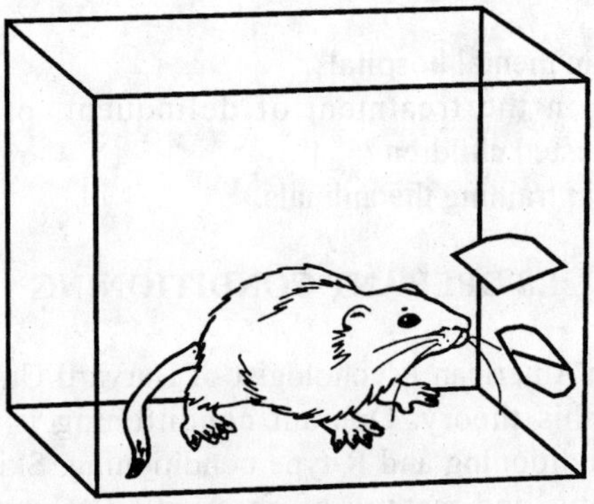

Fig. Rat in Skinner Box

Experiment

Skinner developed a box called Skinner box to conduct his studies. A hungry rat is placed inside the box. In the box there was a lever which is connected to a food container. When the lever is pressed, food pellet is dropped on the plate which was placed near to the lever. While moving around, pawing the wall, the hungry rat accidently presses the lever and a food pellet drops on the plate which the rat eats. The rat continues exploring. He presses the lever and gets the food. After some trials, the rat learns to press the lever and gets the food without any difficulty. Now the behaviour is learned by the rat through its consequences. In this experiment lever pressing is an operant behaviour and getting food is the consequence.

In another experiment with pigeon, a hungry pigeon is put in the pigeon box. The pigeon had to raise head to a particular height and peck at a particular spot in order to get food.

Fig.: Pigeon in a Skinner Box

In operant conditioning the important stimulus (known to the organism) is the one which immediately following the response. This stimulus is known as reinforcement. Any emitted response or operant response which leads to reinforcement is thereby strengthened.

Principle of Operant Conditioning

The law of operant conditioning is that if the occurrence of an operant is followed by presentation of a reinforcing stimulus, then its strength (the probability to occur) increases. Some of the important operations involved in operant conditioning are as follows:

(i) Concept of Reinforcement
(ii) Shaping
(iii) Extinction
(iv) Spontaneous Recovery

Reinforcement is an important concept used by Skinner to explain the theory of operant conditioning.

Concept of Reinforcement

A reinforcer is defined as any stimulus or event, which increases the probability of occurrence of a response. It raise the rate of responding.

Types of Reinforcement

(1) *Positive Reinforcement:* Positive reinforcement involves any pleasant stimuli, the presentation of which increases the probability or occurrence of a response. Positive reinforcement satisfies the needs which includes food, water, reward, praise or money etc. In positive reinforcement organisms do something (desired action) to get something (positive reinforcement).

(2) *Negative Reinforcement:* Negative reinforcement is an unpleasant stimuli, which increases the probability of response. One learns to move away from dangerous stimuli because they provide negative reinforcement. Examples of negative reinforcement are disapproval of parents, teachers or friends etc. In negative reinforcement, organism does something (desirable behaviour or action) to avoid something (negative reinforcement).

It may be noted that negative reinforcement is not any kind of corporal punishment. Punishment suppresses or reduces the response or behaviour whereas negative reinforcement increases the probability desired response. The effect of punishment is not permanent. Sometimes due to punishment, the punished person may develop dislike and hatred for the person who administers the punishment.

Type of Reinforcement Schedule

A reinforcement schedule is the arrangement or procedure of giving reinforcement during conditioning. Reinforcement schedule can be continuous or intermittent. Some types of schedule are as follows:

(1) *Continuous Reinforcement Schedule:* In this type of schedule, reinforcement is provided after every correct response. At the acquisition stage of learning this type of schedule is used.

(2) *Fixed Interval Reinforcement Schedule:* In a fixed interval reinforcement schedule, reinforcement is given after a set interval of time. For example, after a set interval of 5 minutes, half an hour, one hour etc., response of the organism is reinforced. Getting salary at a fixed interval of time is an example of fixed interval reinforcement schedule.

(3) *Fixed Ratio Schedule:* When reinforcement is given after a fixed number of responses, it is called fixed ratio schedule. For example, after answering a fixed number of questions, the learner is reinforced or a man is paid after a certain amount of work.

(4) *Variable Interval Schedule:* In this type of schedule, reinforcement is provided at varying interval of time. The learner does not know when he/she will be reinforced. Therefore, the organism develops a steady rate of response.

(5) *Variable Ratio Reinforcement Schedule:* When reinforcement is given after a varying number of responses, it is called variable ratio reinforcement schedule.

After discussing all the above reinforcement schedules we can conclude that during the acquisition stage or for a beginner, continuous reinforcement schedule is important but after some time when the reinforcement is stopped, then extinction of response takes place i.e. learning of response is forgotten when reinforcement is stopped. If variable schedule reinforcement is used, greater is resistance to extinction.

Shaping

Shaping techniques of operant conditioning is useful for acquisition of complex behaviour and learning of difficult skills. Shaping refers to the judicious use of selective reinforcement to modify the behaviour. In this technique every successful step of the learner towards the goal is reinforced. It can be understood with the help of an experiment. In one experiment, Skinner wants to train a pigeon to walk in a figure Eight (8). Firstly, all the initial activities of a pigeon were watched, then a reinforcement (small amount of grain) was given for simply turning its head in the right direction. Then reinforcement is given for taking a step in the right direction. Thus pigeon learn to move on the required path. Here all the successful steps closer to the goal are reinforced. This technique is very useful to learn complex and difficult task: "teaching spelling is mainly a process of shaping complex form of behaviour".

Extinction

Extinction means the disappearance of learned response due to the removal of reinforcement when the appropriate response occurs. Removal or withholding the reinforcement means extinction of previously established relationship. For example, if lever pressing in Skinner box is not followed by food pellet, the learned behaviour will gradually be weakened and ultimately disappear.

Learning shows resistance to extinction. It means that even though the learned response is not reinforced, it would continue to occur for some time. However, with increasing number of trials without reinforcement, the response gradually disappears and ultimately stops occurring.

Spontaneous Recovery

Spontaneous recovery occurs after a learned response is extinguished. If an organism learns a response in a situation for getting reinforcement, the response can be extinguished by removing the reinforcement. It has been demonstrated that after sometime when the organism is returned in the same situation and reinforcement is given again, his performance is better than his performance at the end of preceding extinction. The amount of spontaneous recovery depends on the duration of time lapsed after the extinction session. Longer the duration of time lapsed, greater the recovery of learned responses.

Educational Implications of Operant Conditioning Theory

The educational implications of operant conditioning theory are as follows:

(1) *Useful in behaviour modification:* Behaviour of an organism can be modified by using the shaping techniques. To shape the behaviour or modify it, reinforcement should be used appropriately by the teacher. Behaviour can be shaped through successive approximation in terms of small steps. Successive approximation is a process in which complex behaviour can be shaped by systematically reinforcing closer approximations to the desired behaviour. It means that every successful step of child must be reinforced by the teacher, instead of waiting for the complete behaviour.

(2) *Useful in developing human personality*: Skinner said, "we are what we have been rewarded for being. What we call personality is nothing more than consistent behaviour patterns that summarise our reinforcement history". We learn any behaviour or language because we have been rewarded for all approximation related to that behaviour or language.

(3) *Importance of reinforcement:* Reinforcement is the centre point of operant conditioning theory. To train or learn behaviour, teacher should have complete knowledge of all types of reinforcement and reinforcement schedules. Apart from the knowledge he/she should judiciously use the reinforcement.

(4) *Avoidance of punishment:* According to this theory, punishment suppresses the behaviour. The effect of punishment is not permanent. When threat of punishment is removed, original behaviour returns. Therefore, this theory emphasises on using positive and negative reinforcement rather than punishment to shape the behaviour.

(5) *Basis for programmed instruction and teaching machines:* On the basis of basic principle of operant conditioning B.F. Skinner develops a system of learning known as programmed instruction. This model is popularly known as 'Linear Model of Programmed Instruction'.

Programmed instruction is the process of arranging the material to be learned into a series of sequential steps. Usually it moves the learner from a familiar background into complex and new set of concepts, principles and understanding. The basic principles of programmed instructions like principle of small steps of content, principle of active responding of learner and principle of immediate reinforcement (by giving information about the result) based upon operant conditioning.

(6) *Teaching-learning activities should be organised:* Teaching-learning activities should be organised in proper manner. There should be provision of immediate reinforcement after completing a task.

Difference between Classical and Operant Conditioning

Classical Conditioning	*Operant Conditioning*
1. Classical conditioning was developed by I.P. Pavlov, a Russian Psychologist.	It was developed by B.F. Skinner.
2. It is related to respondent behaviour.	It is related to operant behaviour.
3. Classical conditioning is stimulus oriented. It is called S-type conditioning as emphasis is given on the importance of stimulus in eliciting desired response.	Operant conditioning is response oriented, and it is called R-type as emphasis is on response.
4. The essence of learning is stimulus-substitution.	The essence of learning is response modification.
5. In it there is pairing of unconditioned stimulus and conditioned stimulus (UCS and CS).	There is no pairing of UCS and CS, but pairing of a response and the reinforcing stimulus which follows.
6. Reinforcement comes first as in Pavlov's experiment food is presented (or visible) first to elicit the response.	Reinforcement is provided after the response is made by organism.
7. Classical conditioning focusses on the single (S-R) Stimulus-Response Bondage.	Operant conditioning is concerned with sequence of responses for desired behaviour. A chain by responses is formed which leads to desired goal.
8. More useful in language learning, treatment of delinquent, problem and maladjusted child.	More useful in behaviour modification.

1.9 INSIGHT THEORY OF LEARNING
Or
GESTALT THEORY OF LEARNING

Insight theory of learning is also known as Gestalt theory of learning. Max Wentheimer is generally considered to be the founding father of Gestalt psychology. Kurt, Koffka and Waffgang Kohler are the other pioneers in this field.

Gestalt is a German word which means 'configuration', 'form or pattern' or perceived as a whole. According to the Gestalt psychologists, the whole is greater than its parts. We cannot understand anything only by study of its parts. In order to understand it we have to study it in a totality. For example, a flower is a not only the total of sepals, petals, colour, fragrance but something more than that. It is the proper organisation of parts which makes it a whole. According to Gestaltatian's view, learning is the organisation and reorganisation of behaviour which arises from the interaction of an organism with its environment.

Gestalt psychologist is primarily concerned with the nature of perception. Perception means sensation plus meaning. Meaningful interpretation of sensation is called perception. According to it, learner while learning does not perform random activities but perceives a situation as a whole. After seeing and evaluating the relation between different elements of situation, he/she takes the appropriate decision in an intelligent manner. Gestalt psychology stresses that insight is used by the learner while learning. According to the Woodworth, "...insight means a good observation, perception of the situation as a whole or perception of those parts of the solution that provide a route to the goal."

Experiments

Kohlar conducted various experiments on chimpanzees to show learning by insight. His experiment on chimpanzee was divided in four parts:

(1) *In first part chimpanzee named 'Sultan' was put inside a cage and some bananas were suspended from the ceiling.* A box was put inside the cage. The Chimpanzee made several attempts to get banana but could not get it, but after perceiving the whole situation, he suddenly got an idea and used the box by placing it under the hanging bananas and thus got the bananas.

(2) *The other situation was more difficult.* Now the two boxes were put in the cage. The situation was such that if one box was put

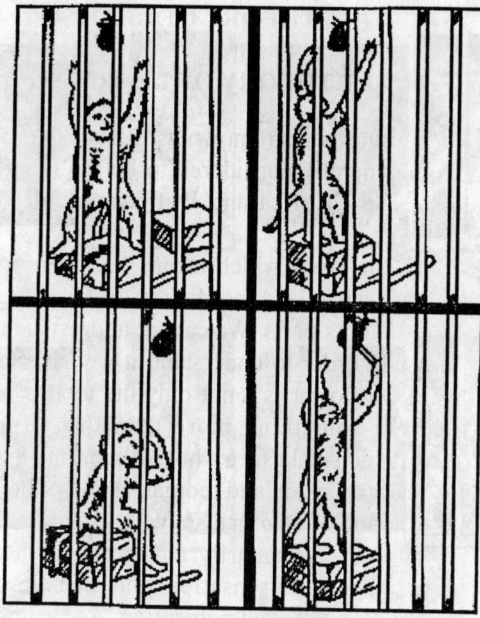

Fig.: Kohler's Experiment on Chim panzee

on top of the other, only then the chimpanzee could get the bananas. First of all, the chimpanzee used a box to get the bananas, but he could not succeed. Finally after perceiving the situation when he maintain relationship between different parts (boxes), he got an idea suddenly. He kept one box over the other and then he achieved the target. So by insight, he solved the problem.

(3) *In third situation chimpanzee was put in a cage and one stick was kept in the cage.* The bananas were placed outside the cage. Firstly, he tried many ways but could not get the bananas. Thereafter, he thought over the whole situation and got an idea. He used the stick and got the bananas.

(4) *The fourth situation was more complicated.* Now two sticks, each too short to reach the banana, were placed in the cage and the bananas were placed outside the cage. The sticks were such that if their ends could be joined together, they would become one. To get the bananas, first of all the chimpanzee used one stick but he failed. Then after some efforts, he perceived the situation as a whole and suddenly got an idea. He took another stick and joined both sticks and picked up the bananas.

With such experiments Kohler concluded that to solve the problem chimpanzee did use trial and error mechanism first. Kohler emphasised on 'suddenness' during trial and error with which the right solution appeared through insight. Learning by insight involves the following criteria:

(1) Initial efforts of insight is through trial and error.
(2) Learning by insight requires complete comprehension of the situation as a whole.
(3) To see and judge the relationship between various components involved in the situation.
(4) The goal must be clear to the learner.
(5) There is new organisation and restructuring of the perceptual field resulting in getting a solution through insight.
(6) The solution flashes suddenly to the learner, through trial and error.
(7) The principle learnt in one situation is applied in another situation.

Factors Influencing Insight

Insight depends upon the following factors:

(i) *Previous experiences:* Experiences are helpful to solve problems. Insightful solution of the problem depends upon the previous experiences of the learner. To solve a new problem or learning of higher level; the previous experiences plays an important role.

(ii) *Intelligence*: Insight will be greater in a more intelligent person, as he can easily perceive the problem as a whole and maintain the relationship between its components effectively.

(iii) *Initial efforts*: The initial efforts are helpful to solve the problem. But this stage does not last long. After some initial efforts, learner uses his insight to solve the problem.

(iv) *Perception of situation:* Without perceiving the situation as a whole and seeing the relationship between the various components of the situation, insightful solution of the problem is not possible.

(v) *Learning situation:* In an arranged learning situation the learner can easily perceive all the aspects of the problem, and solve it easily.

Educational Implication of Insight Theory of Learning

(1) *Presentation of learning material as a whole:* The learning material should be organised and presented in a meaningful whole as this theory emphasises that the 'whole is greater than its parts'. This view can be used in different subjects and concepts as follows:

(a) While teaching various concepts of science as parts of plants or flowers, etc. First of all, the teacher should present a plant or flower as a whole to the student and later on its various parts should be taught. The same method can be applied to teach the various concepts of science as parts of body, various system in human body like digestive system, respiratory system etc. Teacher should use models and charts that show the whole picture at a glance. After that different parts and organs of the body should be taught.

(b) To solve a mathematical problem, first of all it should be presented as a whole to students and then they should be asked to see the different components of the problem and maintain relationship between them. Hence perceiving the problem as a whole a student should solve the problem through his insight. All problems of mathematics should be taught by this method. While teaching geography, teacher should start from the globe or map of the world then come down to country, states, district and city.

(2) *Child as a whole:* Parents and teacher should see the child as a whole; his/her total personality should be taken into account.

(3) *Integrated curriculum:* The curriculum should be integrated. The different subjects and co-curricular activities should be correlated to each other. Also there should be co-relation between different the parts of subjects and among various subjects.

(4) *Importance of transfer:* This theory emphasises the importance of transfer of learning. The teacher should encourage students to use their previous experiences to solve new problem.

(5) *Importance of motivation:* Motivation plays an important role in insightful learning. Teacher should motivate the child. Child should be acquainted well with the aims and purpose of his/her learning.

(6) *Problem solving approach:* The theory train the learner to solve the problem through self effort. It rejects memorisation and rote learning. It stresses that learner must be given opportunity to use their thinking power, power of observation. Why and how in place of what and when should be key-notes of teaching-learning process, through insight.

(7) *Helpful in development of higher mental abilities:* As this theory discards rote learning, the insight learning is helpful in developing and improving higher mental abilities as thinking, imagination, creativity, observation, reasoning, judging, analytical ability and problem solving ability.

1.10 CONCEPTS AND NATURE OF INTELLIGENCE

No two individuals are same. They differ from each other in many aspects. One of the aspect is intelligence. In psychology, intelligence is the general mental ability involved in calculating, reasoning, perceiving relationship, learning quickly, storing and retrieving information, fluency in expression, generalising and adjusting to new situations. It is generally accepted that intelligence is related to both heredity and environment. Both are responsible for an individual's level of intelligence.

Meaning and Definitions of Intelligence

Many attempts have been made by various psychologists to define the term 'Intelligence'. These definition can be divided into three categories.

Intelligence as:

(1) Ability to adjust: The definitions of this category lay emphasis on the adjustment ability of an individual to one's environment. According to this view, intelligence is the ability to adapt and adjust to new situation. A person who is intelligent has no difficulty in the adjustment to new situation. The definitions given by Stern, Calvin, Cruz, Woodworth and many other come under this category. Some of them are as follows:

(i) *Stern:* Intelligence is a general capacity of an individual to consciously adjust his thinking with new requirements. It is general mental adaptability to new problems of life.
(ii) *Woodworth:* Intelligence means intellect put to use. It is the use of intellectual abilities for handling a situation or accomplishing any task.

Intelligence as:

(2) Ability to learn: According to this category, intelligence is the ability to learn. Learning ability is an indicator of one's intelligence.

Buckingham, Dearborn, Calvin and some others belong to this category. Some definitions are as follows:

(i) *According to Buckingham.* "Intelligence is the ability to learn".
(ii) *According to Dearborn's view.* "Intelligence is the capacity to learn or profit by experiences".

Intelligence as:

(3) Ability to carry on abstract thinking: Definitions of this category lay more emphasis on the effective use of concepts and symbols or abstract ideas in dealing with situations. Spearmen, Termen, Binet, Bust and other represent this group.

(i) *Terman view:* An individual is intelligent in proportion as he is able to carry on abstract thinking.

(ii) *Burt's view:* Intelligence is the ability to judge well, to comprehend well and reason well.

Besides all these definitions some comprehensive definitions are as follows:

David Wechsler: "Intelligence is the aggregate or global capacity of the individual to act purposefully, to think rationally and to deal effectively with his environment".

Stoddard's View: Intelligence is the ability to undertake activities that are characterised by (1) difficulty, (2) complexity, (3) abstraction, (4) economy, (5) adaptiveness to a goal, (6) social value, and (7) emergence of originals and to maintain such activities under conditions that demand a concentration on energy and resistance to emotional forces".

On the basis of all these definitions, the following are some characteristics of intelligence.

(1) *Innate power:* Intelligence is an innate and natural power.

(2) *Intelligence is the product of heredity and environment:* Heredity and environment, both are necessary for the intellectual growth of an individual.

(3) *Varies from individual to individual:* Each individual has different intellectual levels. On the basis of their IQ (intelligence quotient) individuals are categorised as genius, superior. above average, average, backward, mentally challenged etc.
The distribution of intelligence governed by a definite principle i.e. the majority of the person, lies at average level—few are very bright and others are very dull.

(4) *Intelligence and sex difference*: Various studies shows that there is no difference in intelligence due to difference in sex.

(5) *Development of intelligence is very rapid for the first six years*

(6) Development of intelligence reaches its maximum, in majority of cases at the age of 16 to 18 years.

(7) Convergent thinking is the basis of intelligence.

(8) Intelligence is helpful in learning things and making adjustment.

(9) It helps to face and solve complicated and difficult problems and situations.

1.11 CONVERGENT THINKING

The term 'convergent thinking' is given by J.P. Guilford. Generally convergent thinking means the ability of giving one 'correct' answer to standard question. Bringing facts and data together from various sources and then applying knowledge and logic to solve problem and make decisions is known as thinking convergently. It is about learning facts, following instructions and solving problems with one right answer. Most of school curriculum and assessment rely on convergent thinking as the school requires students to gather and remember information and make logical decisions and answer accordingly rather than to seek variety of different creative answers. It is opposite to divergent thinking. It is a type of thinking which focuses on a single well established answer to a problem. It is most effective in the situation where an answer already exists and there is need to recall it. Various types of objective questions—recall and recognition type questions—are associated with this type of thinking.

Convergent thinking emphasise on speed, accuracy and logic. A convergent thinker usually tries to accumulate knowledge that can be applied in future situations. Previously acquired information and a logical thought process is essential for convergent thinking.

Convergent thinking can be presented as:

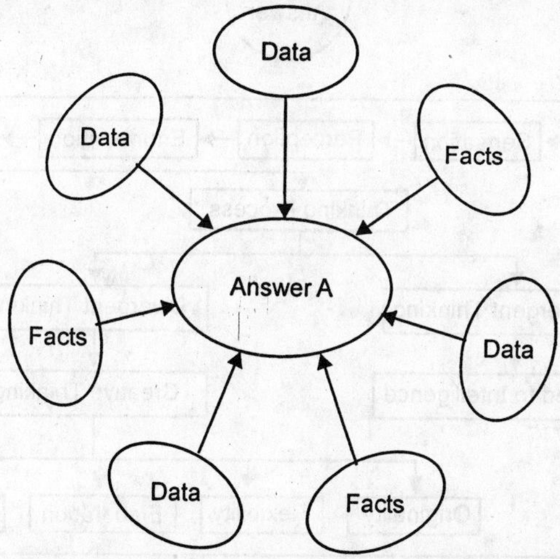

1.12 DIVERGENT THINKING

Divergent Thinking is a thought process or method used to generate creative ideas by exploring many possible solutions. It is opposite to convergent thinking that focuses on a single well established answer to a problem. In divergent thinking many solutions are explored and unexpected connections are drawn. Divergent thinking is an important aspect of creativity where a variety of solutions of a problem are encouraged. Divergent thinking can be presented as:

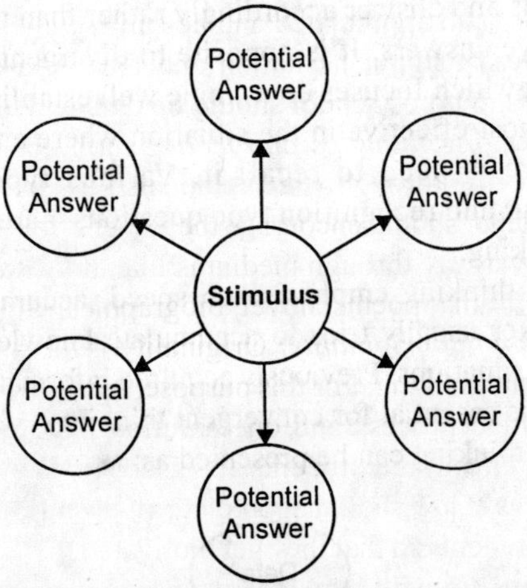

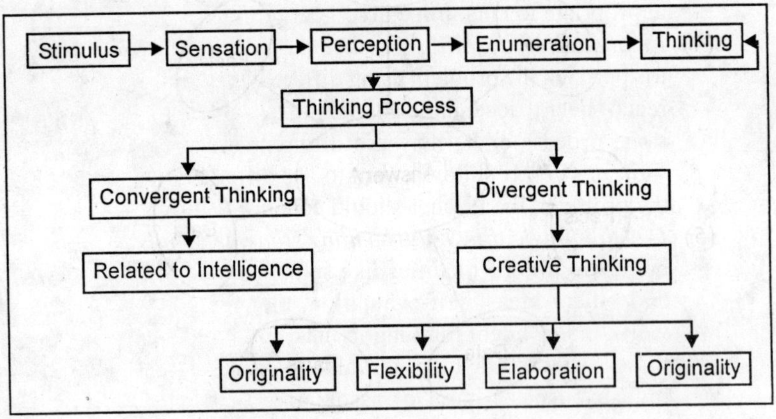

Strategies to Nurture Divergent Thinking

One of the main aims of education is to encourage and promote creativity among students. Some strategies are discussed here which can be used by the teacher to nurture divergent thinking or creativity among students.

(1) *Creating an encouraging environment:* To foster divergent thinking, the school, classroom and home climate should be encouraging. The child should be free to express himself/herself. Teacher and parents should make the student feel that he is accepted and appreciated and he can ask questions, present his new ideas without hesitation and fear. Also the discipline of school and home school should be democratic in nature.

(2) *Encouraging thoughts and feeling in many media:* There are many media through which students can show their creativity. The teacher should encourage the students to express themselves in a novel way through mediums like, art, craft, debate, music, dance, drama, poems, novel, biographies, etc.

(3) *Encouraging originality:* Originality is an important aspect of divergent thinking. For this purpose, teacher should not demand the routine process and one solution of a problem. Teachers should encourage students to discover new ways of solving problems. They should appreciate all the new and original ideas of the students so that they get motivated to think independently and come up with new ideas. Open ended situations are most appropriate to encourage divergent thinking.

(4) *Emphasis on flexibility.* Teacher should encourage the students to approach the problem using different methods. A student may reach several acceptable answers to a problem by following the same process or he may use different processes to reach the same answer. If children want to use different methods to solve the problem, the teacher should encourage it.

(5) *Developing healthy habits among students:* Children should be helped to imbibe qualities like self-trust, respect for their own and others ideas, self-evaluation, concentration, devotion to work, independent thinking in making judgments, figuring out things without any help, visualising causes and consequences, industriousness, habit of associative thinking etc. All these qualities are helpful in creative output.

(6) *Being a creative person oneself.* Teacher should be the role model for their children. Teacher should be creative in his/her methods and work procedure. Creative learning required creative teaching. The teacher should present the problem before the students creatively. As far as possible, teacher should allow students to work out the problem independently with little guidance. The discovery method and constructivistic approach should be encouraged appropriately.

(7) *Rewarding creative achievement.* Torrance suggested five ways in which teacher can reward creative achievement:

(i) Treat unusual questions which the children ask with respect.

(ii) Treat unusual ideas and solutions with respect.

(iii) Appreciate children's ideas.

(iv) Provide opportunity and give credit for self-initiated learning.

(v) Provide chance to think, discover without threats of immediate achievement.

(8) *Reform in evaluation system.* Our evaluation system is mostly based on memorising the various concepts. There should be provision for creativity in our evaluation system.

(9) *Organisation of curriculum:* The curriculum should be organised in such a manner that it will satisfy the need of children. Various subjects and co-curricular activities should be so designed as to foster creativity among students. It should be based on concept rather than facts. There should be variety of subjects and activities in the curriculum, so that students can choose according to their interest and ability.

(10) *Using creative resources of the community.* Resources of community can be used in two ways. Firstly, creative persons from different fields and sections of the society may be invited to school. Secondly, children should be taken to the center of creative art, industry where some creative process is used to make creative product.

(11) *Use of special techniques.*

(i) *Brain storming.* This technique was developed by Osborn. It is a technique which emphasises the importance of divergent thinking. It is based on the principle that producing ideas should be kept separate from the evaluation of their worth. The basic assumption is to let the minds think freely and the tendency to judge the worthiness of ideas may be postponed: Here, a particular problem is proposed for discussion. For example. What other changes you want in your school or what could be the other uses of objects (ruler, comb, spoon, etc.). Students are asked to express their views with full freedom of expression. All ideas are encouraged and appreciated. No idea is criticised. When all ideas are received, they should be discussed in free, frank and congenial environment. The ideas that are most suitable should be accepted for solving the problems in consideration.

(ii) *Use of teaching models.* Suchman's inquiring training model and Bruner's concept attainment model are helpful in developing creativity.

(iii) *Use of gaming techniques.* Some gaming techniques are helpful in developing creative ability. These could be in the form of solving riddles, puzzles, mystries, building blocks, making objects from waste material, etc.

(iv) *Role play techniques.* During the role play, students reflect, express their creativity freely. Whatever role allotted to them they justify their talent of creativity.

1.13 MULTIPLE INTELLIGENCE

"Intelligence is the ability to solve problems, or to create products, that are valued within one or more cultural settings".

— *Howard Gardner*

Howard Gardner was born in Scrlaton, Pennsylvania USA in 1943. He is a psychologist and professor at Harvard University's graduate school of education. Gardner first outlined his theory of multiple intelligence in his book 'Frames of Mind' in 1983. This theory of multiple intelligence challenged the traditional beliefs in the field of education that 'intelligence is a uniform cognitive capacity, people are born with, and can be easily measured by IQ tests, and its level does not change over a life time.' Gardner claims that all human beings have multiple intelligence. These multiple intelligence can be nurtured and strengthened.

According to Gardner:

- All human being possess all nine intelligence in varying amount.

- Each individual has a different intellectual compositions.
- We can improve education by addressing the multiple intelligence of our students.
- These intelligence are located in different areas of the brain and can either work independently or together.

Gardner initially formulated a list of seven types of intelligence and later on added two more in this series.

(1) Linguistic intelligence	Typically valued in school
(2) Logical-mathematical intelligence	
(3) Bodily-kinaesthetic intelligence	Associated with art
(4) Musical intelligence	
(5) Spatial-visual intelligence	
(6) Interpersonal intelligence	Personal intelligence
(7) Intrapersonal intelligence	

Out of these types of intelligence, the first two have been typically valued in schools, the next three are usually associated with the arts and the final two types are personal intelligence.

After subsequent researches and reflections by Howard Gardner and his colleagues two more types of intelligence were added:

(8) Naturalistic intelligence
(9) Existential intelligence

(1) ***Linguistic Intelligence:*** It involves sensitivity to spoken and written language, the ability to learn language and the capacity to use language to accomplish certain goals. This type of intelligence includes the ability to effectively use language to express oneself, and language as a means to remember information. Writers, poets, lawyers, journalists and speakers, etc. have high linguistic intelligence.

(2) ***Logical-mathematical Intelligence:*** This type of intelligence is related to the capacity to analyse problems logically, carry out mathematical operations and investigate issues scientifically. According to Gardner, it entails the ability to detect patterns, reason deductively and think logically. This intelligence in most often associated with scientific and mathematical thinking. This type of intelligence is visible

in professionals like scientists, engineers, mathematicians, accountants, statisticians, analysts, etc.

(3) ***Bodily-kinaesthetic Intelligence:*** It involves the control of one's bodily motions and the capacity to handle objects skillfully. People who have good bodily-kinaesthetic intelligence are generally good at physical activities such as sports, dance, acting, etc. This type of intelligence is oftenly associated with athletes, dancers, actors, police officers, soldiers, etc.

(4) ***Musical Intelligence:*** It encompasses the capacity to recognise and compose musical pitches, tones and rhythms. This type of intelligence is visible in quite a large proportion in professionals like musicians and music composers, singers, musical instrument operators, etc.

(5) ***Spatial-visual Intelligence:*** It deals with the interpretation and creation of visual images, pictorial imagination and expression. The person having this intelligence can understand relationship between images and meaning and space and effect. Artists, architects, photographers, engineers, designers and other associated professionals have high spatial-visual intelligence.

(6) ***Interpersonal Intelligence:*** It is concerned with the capacity to understand the intensions, motivations, emotions and desires of other people. It allows people to work effectively with others. Educators, sales person, political leaders, social workers and counsellors, all need a well-developed interpersonal intelligence.

(7) ***Intrapersonal Intelligence:*** It consists of an individual's abilities to know own self. It includes knowledge of one's own strengths, abilities, emotions, weakness, style, cognitive strengths, etc.

(8) ***Naturalist Intelligence:*** It enables an individual to recognise, categorise and draw upon certain features of the environment, such as ability to recognise and categorise plants, animals and other objects in nature, with their role and use. Botanist, agriculturist, farmers, nature lovers having this intelligence.

(9) ***Existential Intelligence:*** It includes the sensitivity and capacity to tackle deep questions about human existence such as meaning of life, why do we die, where do we go after death, etc. Philosophers and saints having this intelligence.

The table given below indicates each type of intelligence and its description:

Types of Intelligence with Descriptions

Intelligence Type	*Description*	*Roles*
(1) Linguistic	• Sensitivity to written and spoken language • Ability to interpret and explain the ideas and information through language	Writers, speakers, poets, lawyers
(2) Logical-mathematical	• Capacity to discuss logic, or numerical pattern • Carry out mathematical operations and understand relationship between cause and effect	Scientists, mathematicians, accountants, researchers, statisticians
(3) Bodily-kinaesthetic	• Capacity to recognise, appreciate and compose musical pitches, tones and rhythms	Musicians, music composers
(4) Musical	• Ability to interpret and create visual images, pictorial images and expression • Understand the relationship between images and meaning and space & effect	Architects, navigators, sculptors
(5) Spatial-visual	• Abilities to control of one's bodily motion and handle objects skilfully	Athletes, dancers, sports person
(6) Interpersonal	• Capacity to understand the intensions, emotions and drive of other people • Ability to work effectively with others	Sales persons, counsellors, educators, therapists
(7) Intrapersonal	• Capacity to understand one's self	Any person who has detailed accurate self-knowledge
(8) Naturalistic	• Ability to recognise, categorise and draw upon certain features of environment • Deal with natural environment	Botanists, Agricultarists, Farmers, Nature lovers
(9) Existential	• Capability and sensitivity to tackle deep questions about human existence	Saints, philosophers

Implications of Multiple Intelligence

Educational implications of multiple intelligence can be discussed under the following points:

(1) *Students become more active like involved learner:* If a teacher has knowledge about all types of intelligence then he/she will provide opportunities for authentic learning based on students' needs, interests, talents etc. The students will also become more active and take better interest in learning.

(2) *Useful to develop personality of the students:* If students will get learning opportunities according to their need and interest, they will be able to demonstrate and share their strengths. Building strengths gives students the motivation to be 'specialists'.

(3) *Use a wide variety of ways to present the lesson/topic:* With the knowledge of all types of intelligence, the teacher should present the lesson/topic in a wide variety of ways. He/she should use music, cooperative learning, activities, role play, multimedia, field trips, project method etc.

(4) *Identifying talented children in their specified fields:* The knowledge of different types of intelligence gives opportunity to a teacher to identify various talents in children with the help of various psychological techniques and methods.

2
Determinants and Process of Learning

2.0 NEED

Need is necessary for an organism to live a healthy life. Generally, it is lack of something. To most psychologists, need is a condition, situation or state of mind that arouses an organism to act towards the goal, giving purpose and direction to one's behaviour. The term 'need' is used in many ways in our daily life. For example, we need rest when we are tired; we need water for quenching our thirst; when we are hungry, we need food and sometime we need appreciation or recognition for our work.

"Need is a condition or situation in which something must be supplied in order for a certain condition to be maintained or a desired state to be achieved".

2.1 TYPES OF NEED

Need may be of many types as biological need, social need, need for esteem, repect, esteem etc. Regarding the types of needs, **Maslow,** the famous psychologist developed the hierarchy model of needs. This hierarchy is often displayed as a pyramid. The lowest level of pyramid is made up of the most basic needs, while the more complex and higher order needs are located at the top of the pyramid. There are five levels of hierarchy of needs which are given below:

1. Physiological Needs

These include most basic needs that are vital for human survival, such as need of food, water, air, sleep, sex etc. If these needs are not fulfilled or met, the human body cannot function properly and will ultimately fail. Maslow believed that these needs are most basic and instinctive needs in the hierarchy because all needs become secondary until these psychological needs are met.

2. Security Needs

Once physiological needs are met, one's attention turns to safety and security in order to feel free from threat of physical and emotional harm. These are the needs connected with the psychological fear of loss of job, property, natural climate and hazard. Examples of security needs include job security, safe neighbourhood, personal security, safety against accidents and medical insurance in illness, life insurance policies, etc. According to Maslow, if a person feels threatened, then he/she will not pay attention on the needs of next upper level.

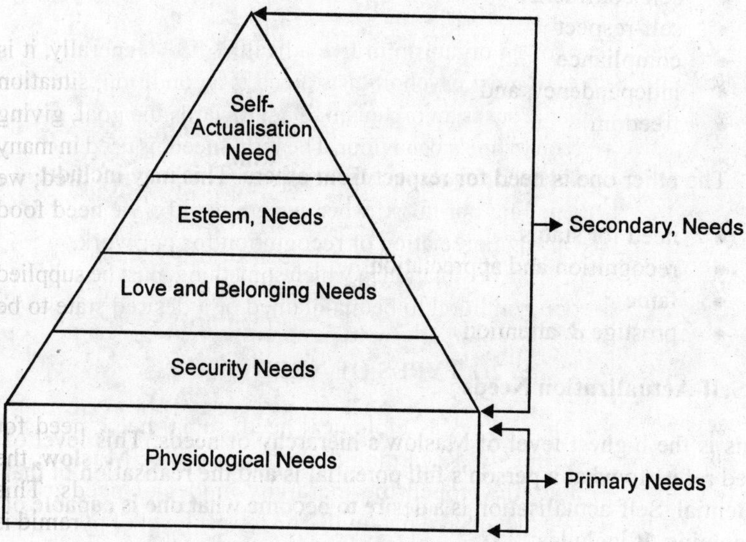

Fig.: Maslow's Hierarchy Model of Needs

3. Love and Belongingness Needs

When one feels secure and is satisfied with the physiological needs, one can think of satisfaction of next level of needs i.e., love and belongingness need. Every person feels that he should belong to one or other group and the member of the group should accept him with love and affection. These needs include:

- friendship
- belonging to a group

- giving and receiving love
- intimacy
- affection and love from family, friends and groups

4. Esteem Needs

All human have a need to feel respected, to be accepted and valued by others. Once the previous needs are fulfilled, a person feels to be held in esteem both by himself and also by others. Therefore, these needs are two fields in nature. The first one is the self-esteem need which includes:

- self-confidence
- self-respect
- compliance
- independency, and
- freedom

The other one is need for respect from others. This may include:

- need for status
- recognition and appreciation
- fame
- prestige & attention

5. Self-Actualization Needs

This is the highest level of Maslow's hierarchy of needs. This level of need refers to what a person's full potential is and the realisation of that potential. Self-actualisation is a desire to become what one is capable of becoming. It includes:

- realising personal potential
- self-fulfilment
- seeking personal growth and
- peak experiences

Implications of Needs

The knowledge of all types of need are very important for the persons associated with education process:

1. Helpful to Understand the Child

If teachers as well as parents are aware about the different needs of a child, then they can understand the child better. For example, if a child is tired and hungry, it is difficult for him/her to focus on learning and all efforts made by teachers and parents would be wasted. Also if the child is emotionally and physically safe and accepted in the home and classroom, she/he will learn effectively and attentively and reach full potential.

2. Give Value and Respect to the Student's View and Personality

Students must be shown that they and their views are valued and respected in the classroom and teacher should create a supportive environment. Students with a low self-esteem will not progress academically until their self-esteem is strengthened.

3. Provide Motivation According to Need of Students

Everyone has his own need; one's is not motivated by the same needs. Teacher should recognise the learners need and motivate them accordingly. For example, young children need love, security (emotional and physical) etc. Elders need praise, recognition, acceptance, attention. Therefore, teacher should motivate students according to their needs.

2.2 INTEREST

Each individual has some interest; only due to interest, he like objects, activities, etc. It is an important factor in achievement. Interests give us pleasure, satisfaction and create enthusiasm. Interests are shaped by heredity and environment both. They are learnt and become less varied with increasing age.

Some definitions of interest are as follows:

According to Murphy: "Interests are conditioned stimuli related to goal objects and expressed as likes or dislikes of activities, objects or characteristics of people in the environment".

According to Buckingham: "An interest is a tendency to become absorbed in an experience and to continue it".

Role of Teacher to Promote and Arouse Interest or Ways of Promoting and Arousing Interest

1. Determination of proper objectives.

2. Use of child-centred method of teaching and learning as project method, play-way method, activity method, constructivist approach, etc.
3. Use of audio-visual aids.
4. Linking previous knowledge to new knowledge.
5. Linking the knowledge with daily life of students.
6. Awareness among the students about the purpose and objectives of topic/knowledge.
7. Making environment of the classroom healthy and democratic.
8. Content should be logically and psychologically arranged.
9. Content should be Meaningful and interesting.
10. Content and activities should be according to the mental level of students.
11. Timetable should be according to learner's mental age; and subjects should be logically arranged in the time-table.

Importance of Interest in Education

Knowledge of interest is very important for a teacher. It helps the teacher in many ways:

1. ***To make teaching-learning process effective (use of effective method of teaching):*** If the teacher teaches according to the interests of the students, they will pay more attention in learning and learning will be effective and permanent.
2. ***Helpful to save time and energy:*** If the child learns anything with interest, it saves time and energy of both student and teacher, and also learning will be long lasting.
3. ***Helpful to maintain discipline in class:*** Mostly indiscipline is created in class where students are not interested in learning. Interesting learning is helpful in maintaining discipline as students pay more attention.
4. ***Helpful in increasing attention and concentration of learner:*** If the learning is interesting, it automatically increases attention and concentration of learner in learning.
5. ***Helpful to achieve the objectives of education:*** Objectives of education can be easily achieved if students take interest in classroom teaching.

2.3 ATTITUDE

One of the main objectives of education is to develop attitude among students. An individual's behaviour is largely dependent upon his/her attitude towards the people, things, ideas, objects etc. Also learning of a subject, acquisition of habits, interest etc. are all affected by the attitude. It is important for a teacher to understand the meaning of attitude.

Definition of Attitude

According to James Travers: "An attitude is a readiness to respect in such a way that behaviour is given a certain direction."

According to Thurston: "Attitude denotes the sum total of man's inclinations and feelings, prejudice or bias, pre-conceived notion, ideas, fears, threats about any specific topic."

In Karen Honrey view: "Attempting or tendency cheer to move towards, against or away from a person, object or situation."

From these definitions it may be concluded that attitude is a point of view or opinion toward a subject, thing, object, idea or person. It may be positive or negative. It is a tendency or predisposition to behave in a particular and definite way to a particular situation. One's attitude decides one's response to a particular situation.

Characteristics of Attitude

1. Attitudes are learned.
2. Attitudes manifest in behaviour.
3. Attitudes have motivational properties.
4. Attitude involves direction as well as magnitude.
5. Attitude ranges from strongly positive to strongly negative.

Importance of Attitude in Education

It is very important to inculcate the desirable attitude and eliminate the undesirable one among students. Attitude is important in education in these ways:

- To develop proper social attitude, i.e. desirable attitude towards the society and those among the students.
- To achieve the objective of education, desirable attitude of learner is important.

- To save time and energy, desirable attitude is must.
- To succeed in life, correct and positive attitude is essential.
- Positive attitude helps to bring optimism and motivates towards success.

How to Develop Correct Attitude among Children

- Attitudes are caught through direct or indirect experiences. Therefore teacher should make use of indirect suggestions, provide experiences that will naturally tend to result in desired attitude.
- Teachers and family members should be free from undesirable attitudes.
- To develop favourable attitude towards subject, the teacher should use proper teaching methods and provide good experiences to students.

2.4 MOTIVATION

A seven year old child, who wants to learn roller-skating, despite many failures and minor injuries, continues to learn it. A girl of poor family continues her learning 14 to 16 hours, to get success in medical exams. These examples indicate the role of motivation in human behaviour. Motivation explains the 'why and how of human behaviour?' Motivation includes all those activities which are responsible for arousing, sustaining & regulating our activities towards the goal. Now we will discuss the meaning and definition of motivation.

Motivation is derived from Latin word **'movere'** which means **'to move'**. Literally, motivation is the process of arousing movement in the organism. It is a force which compels an individual to act or to behave in a particular direction.

Some other definitions of motivation are given below:

(i) According to **Johnson**, "Motivation is the influence of general pattern of activities indicating and directing behaviour of the organism".

(ii) **Atkinson** says, "The term motivation refers to the arousal of a tendency to act, to produce one or more effects".

(iii) According to **Guilford**. "Motivation is an internal fact or condition that tends to initiate and sustain activity".

The motivational cycle

The different aspects of motivation are need, drive, goal, incentive. Motivation constitutes a cycle completed in different stages which are as follows:

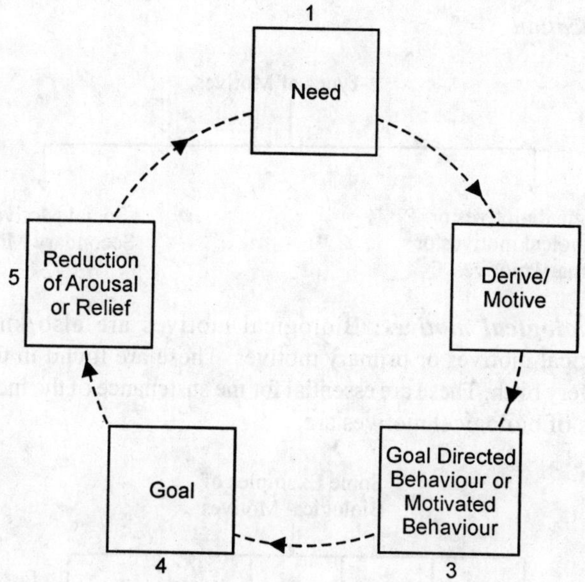

The cycle can be explained as:

(i) The starting point of the motivation cycle is birth of need, desire or want in individual. A need is lack or deficit of some necessity. This need makes the individual to think about the ways and means of its satisfaction. The condition of need leads to drive.

(ii) Drive or motives is a state of tension or arousal produced by need. It energises one's behaviour and action. It initiates one's behaviour to a goal directed path.

(iii) With the help of motivated behaviour, individual is able to realise the desired goal and feel satisfied. It enables him to get relief from the anxiety and tension and he returns to a psychologically and physiologically balanced state.

Types of Motives

There are number of motives in our personal and social life which are responsible for energising and motivating our behaviour. Many psychologists have classified the motives in different types:

I. Classification

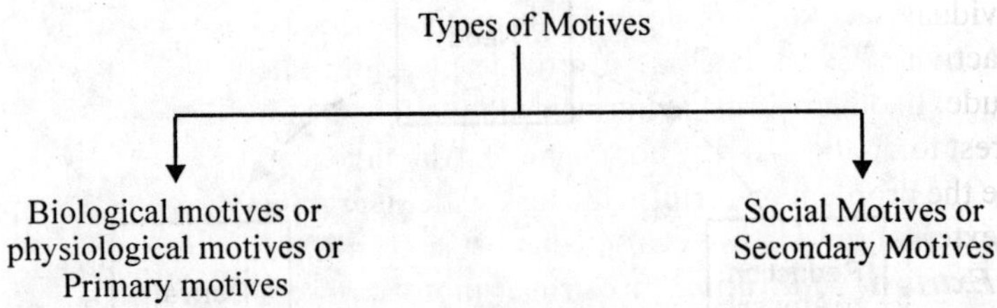

1. *Biological motives*: Biological motives are also known as physiological motives or primary motives. These are found in the child from the very birth. These are essential for the sustenance of the individual. Examples of biological motives are:

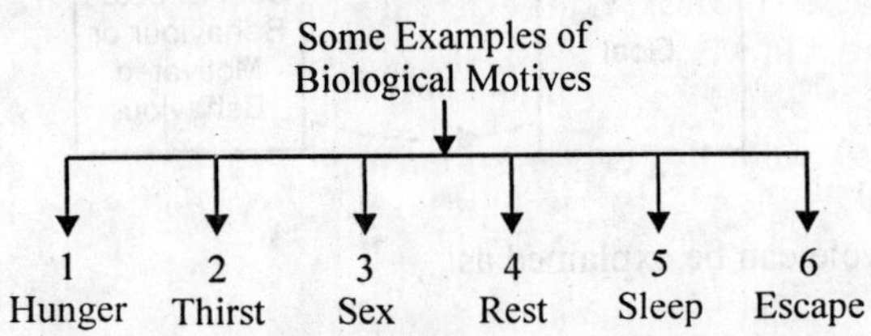

2. *Sociological motives*: Social motives are called secondary motives. Man's cultural heritage and philosophy of life influence these social motives.

Some examples of social motives:

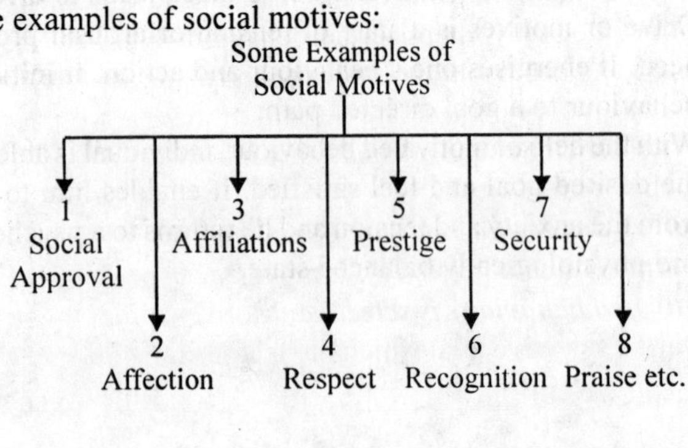

II. Other Classifications

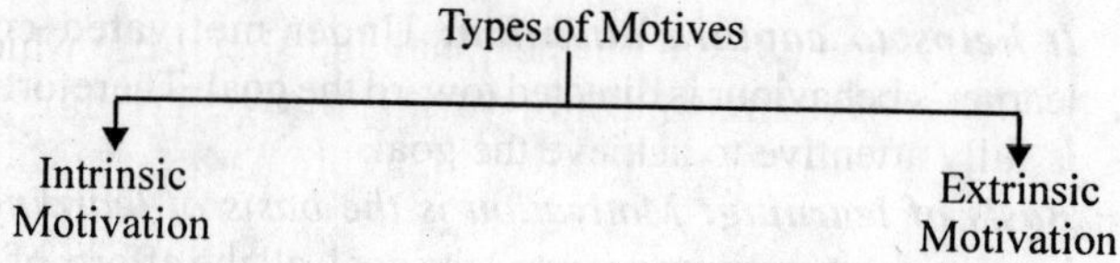

Intrinsic Motivation: It is a type of motivation due to which an individual is naturally or intrinsically motivated to do a task. He performs the activity or task because it provide pleasure, interest or favourable attitude. In other words, in intrinsic motivation an individual has his own interest to do the activity. For example, when the learner himself tries to solve the problem or perform the task with pleasure and interest without any external reward, we can say that he/she is intrinsically motivated.

Extrinsic Motivation: In extrinsic motivation, learner pursues a task for any reason which are external, either a reward or objectives. Here, the activity or task does not itself give pleasure to him. All tasks or activities are directed with some external motivation.

For example: Learners do assignments or any work due to getting better marks or grades, praise, reward, etc. It means some external factors are involved to do the task. If the external motivation remove learner will not take interest in work.

Role of Motivation in Teaching-Learning Process or Functions of Motivation

Motivation plays an important role in teaching-learning process. Some points are discussed as under:

1. ***Motives energise and sustain behaviour*:** Motives provide energy to the behaviour of the learner and arouse for action. Motives not only energise the behaviour but also sustain our interest and behaviour for longer period in the activity. So motive like rewards, praise etc. are helpful in the learning. According to *Heff*, efficiency and adequacy are increased in motivated state of behaviour.
2. ***Motives direct and regulate behaviour*:** Motivated behaviour is purposeful and persistent. It moves in a specific direction.
3. ***Motivated behaviour is selective*:** Motives direct the behaviour toward a selective goal which the learner sets for himself. They

help the learner in the selection of right responses or activities which are helpful to reach the goal.

4. ***It helps to capture attention:*** Under motivated condition learner's behaviour is directed toward the goal. Therefore, learner is fully attentive to achieve the goal.
5. ***Basis of learning:*** *Motivation is the basis of learning:* If the learner is not motivated toward the goal, all the efforts of teaching are useless. Whereas if the learner is motivated, he/she can learn very efficiently with little guidance or support of teacher. Motives are helpful to achieve the goal of learning.
6. ***Motives are helpful in developing the personality:*** Motivation effect in the development of personality. Learner's personality is dependent upon the motivation provided to him/her from time to time.
7. ***Motives helps in developing feeling of discipline:*** Proper motivation given by the teacher solves the problem of indiscipline among the learners.
8. ***Helpful in developing interest and attitude:*** Before teaching, teacher should motivate students to learn. For this purpose she/he should ask questions related to previous knowledge, tell stories, perform activities to start the topic. If students are ready to learn they will take interest in the teaching-learning process and their attitude will change in desirable direction.

2.5 MEMORY

Memory plays an important role in human life. The success, efficiency and durability of learning to a great extent depends on memory. It preserve our experiences, helps us in solving problems and taking decisions. Memory is central to almost all cognitive processes such as imagination, perception, thinking and problem solving. There is no phase of human living untouched by memory.

Various psychologists have defined memory:

According to ***Stout's:*** Stout has defined memory as "ideal revival" i.e., to revive the things, objects or experiences in the same order and form.

According to ***M.C. Dougal:*** "Memory implies imagining of events as experienced in the past and recognising them to one's own past experiences".

According to ***Ryburn:*** "The power that we have to store our experience and to bring them into the field of consciousness, after some time the experiences have occurred, is termed as memory".

According to ***J.S. Ross:*** "Memory is a complex process involving the establishment of disposition, their retention and recalling of the experiences that have left the deposition behind them".

According to ***Woodworth:*** "Memory consists in remembering what has previously been learned".

In the light of these definitions, it may be concluded that memory is a complex process involving learning, retention, recall and recognition. It is to retain the past experience and reproduction of these experiences from the unconscious mind in the same order and form.

Process of Memory

Four operations involved in the process of memory.

1. Learning
2. Retention
3. Recall
4. Recognition

1. Learning: In order to memorise a thing, the first essential thing is learning. Learning is the acquisition of new experience, new knowledge and modification in behaviour. Anything which is learnt effectively, can be retained for long time. With the role of learning in memory, Guilford says that 'for an efficient memory', effective learning is more than winning half the battle. One must do more than get acquainted with the principles of effective learning. However, in order to have a good memory, one must know when to apply these principles. Furthermore, it always takes some effort to apply.

2. Retention: It is an important part of memory. Retention means preserving the learnt material in mind. After some time the learnt material goes in unconscious mind and gets preserved there. There are some points that can make retention power effective. They are as follows:

(a) The material of learning should be meaningful.
(b) The stimulus should be intense, clear and meaningful.
(c) Those things are remembered well which are learnt by interest and attention, and in good physical & mental health.

(d) More often when an impression occurs is repeated, the deeper it becomes and it is likely to be retained for a longer time than the impression which is not repeated.

(e) The learning by good methods results in better and longer retention than traditional methods.

3. Recall: The third aspect of process of memory is recall. Recall means to revive the past experiences in conscious mind. It requires reproduction of learned material. The material which is retained effectively, can be recalled easily and effectively. On the basis of recall we are able to remember the old things.

4. Recognition: Recognition means to recognise, identify the experiences. It is a capacity to recognise a thing that has been seen earlier. It is the identification of recalled material. In recognition, past experiences are presented to the sense. It is the ability that gives us a signal that we earlier experienced a particular person, thing, phenomenon, picture, etc.

For example, when we meet our friend after many years, we recognise her/him and recall all the things associated with him/her.

Types of Memories

Memory has been categorised in various kinds. Some important types of memories are discussed here:

1. ***Sensory memory:*** The incoming information first enters the sensory memory. Sensory memory has large capacity. However, it is of very short duration. Here information is registered from each of the senses as exact replica of stimulus.

2. ***Short Term Memory (STM)*:** Short term memory holds small amount of information for a brief period of time. It is the immediate recollection of stimuli that is just perceived. When we look at a phone number and just dial, it is the example of STM.

3. ***Long Term Memory (LTM):*** Long term memory has vast capacity. It is paramount house of all informations. It stores large amount of information for a long period of time.

Long term memory can further be classified into:

(a) Declarative memory
(b) Procedural memory

(a) ***Declarative memory*:** All information pertaining to facts, names, dates, such as India got freedom on 15th August, 26th January is our

Memory System

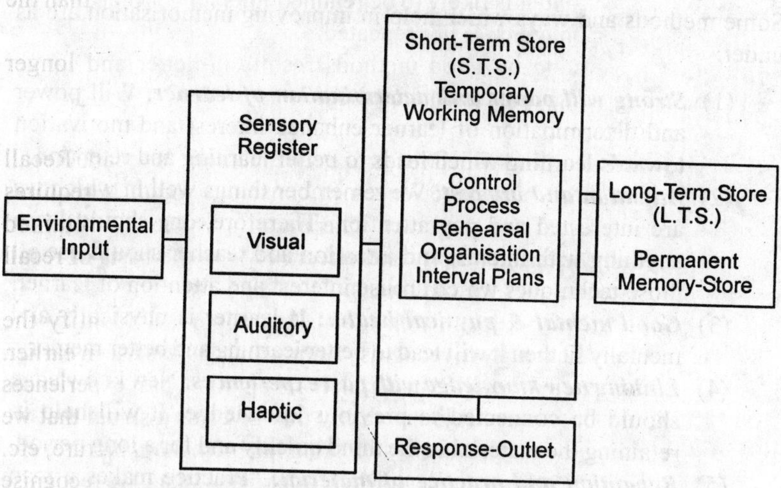

Fig.: Movement of Information within Memory System

republic day, and Mahatma Gandhi is the father of the nation etc. are part of declarative memory.

(b) ***Procedural memory***: Memories related to procedures for accomplishing various tasks and skills are the part of procedural memory. For example, how to ride bicycle? How to play football? How to drive? How to swim? etc.

The content of procedural memory cannot be described easily.

Other classifications of memory by psychologists are:

(i) ***Episodic memory***: It contains the biological details of our lives. It records the personal life experiences of ones' life. For example, when a person remembers how he felt when he stood first in exams. This event is stored in episodic memory.

Although such experiences are hard to forget, there are many events that take place continuously in our lives we do not remember all of them. Besides, there are painful and unpleasant experiences which are not remembered in as much detail as pleasant experiences.

(ii) ***Semantic memory***: It is the memory of general awareness and knowledge. All concepts, ideas and rules are stored in this memory. An example related to this memory is we remember that 8+2 = 10. Similarly, various rules used in maths, grammar, sciences and other subjects etc. are stored in the memory. As the contents of semantic memory are general awareness and knowledge, it is remembered for a long time.

Methods and Techniques of Memorisation

Some methods and ways which help in improving memorisation are as under:

(1) ***Strong will power and determination of learner***: Will power and determination of learner enhance interest and motivation towards learning which leads to better learning and retention.

(2) ***Attention and interest***: We remember things well in which we are interested and pay attention. Therefore, one should learn anything with interest and attention and teacher should use all those techniques which arouse interest and attention of learner.

(3) ***Good mental & physical health***: If learner is physically and mentally fit then it will lead to better learning and better memory.

(4) ***Linking new knowledge with past experiences:*** New knowledge should be connected to previous knowledge. It will help in retaining the material in the mind quickly and for a long period.

(5) ***Repetition and practice of material:*** "Practice makes a man perfect". The learned material should be practiced sufficiently. Also whatever content is taught by the teacher should be revised from time to time. It leads to better retention.

(6) ***Learning by doing:*** Learning experiences acquired through an effort are remembered for longer time. So emphasis should be given on learning by activity. Teacher should plan activity in which he/she can involve the learner for doing some experiments, role play, etc.

(7) ***Meaningful, organised and interesting subject matter:*** In retention, meaningfulness of subject matter is very important. The subject matter should be logically and psychologically organised. It should be interesting and according to the mental level of students.

(8) ***Formation of clear concept with the help of learning aids and methods:*** Another technique to improve memory which a teacher can use is to develop clear concept with the help of various types of audio-visual aid and progressive teaching methods, such as project method, discovery method, problem solving method, demonstration method, play way method, constructivist approach etc. Teacher should try to involve more than one senses in teaching learning process. Active participation helps in improvement of retention also.

(9) ***Provision for rest:*** There should be adequate provision for rest.

Rest removes fatigue, monotony and refreshes the mind of learner. Hence rest should be taken after some time doing work or activity.

(10) ***Use of mnemonic devices:*** We sometime require to learn some complex material. For this, it is useful to use mnemonics devices to retain material. Through this technique, information in the brain is deliberately transformed into meaningful system to improve memory. Some examples of these techniques are:

- pick up first letter of each word we want to remember and arrange them to form another word or sentence. For example colours of rainbow are remembered as VIBGYOR, where V = violet, I = indigo, B = blue, G = green, Y = yellow, O = orange, R = red.
- Another example is of BODMAS: B = bracket, O = of, D = division, M = multiplication, A = addition, S = subtraction

(11) ***Provide motivation:*** Mtivation creates interest, and captures attention, therefore facilitating learning and memorisation.

(12) ***Arranging better teaching situation and environment:*** It includes physical facilities in classroom, methods, attitude of teacher, teaching aid etc. All these are helpful in better memorisation.

(13) ***Making use of SQRRRR (SQ4R) Techniques:*** Thomson and Robinson (1972) have given SQ4R technique. The various steps involved in this technique are as follows:

(i) *Survey*: Initially learner quickly surveys the material to get an idea of what is going to be remembered.

(ii) *Question:* The learner asks himself questions like why, when, what, where and who concerning the material surveyed in the first step.

(iii) *Read*: After this, the material is read for comprehension and for learning the answer to the questions raised in step (ii).

(iv) *Reflecting:* The information given in the required material is organised and made meaningful by:

(a) linking it with the previous knowledge

(b) comparing and contrasting the facts

(c) correlating the information with other similar facts, concepts and principles

(d) attempting to make use of material in solving simulated problems.

(v) *Recite/Recall:* The information provided in the material is remembered through recitation and recall, both orally and in written form.

(vi) *Review:* This is the final step the material required to be remembered is actively reviewed.

The learner asks himself questions related to the information given in the material and in case he/she is unable to provide satisfactory answer, reads the material again, recites and remembers it more carefully and then again evaluates his/her learning or remembering performance.

2.6 FORGETTING

Each one of us have experienced forgetting. Sometimes we fail to recall the name of our friend or some piece of information. In examination or classroom, students fail to recall some important points or concepts. It is all due to forgetting. Many psychologists have defined forgetting as follows:

(1) ***Munn:*** "Forgetting is failing to retain what has been acquired".

Or

"Forgetting is the loss, permanent or temporary, of the ability to recall or recognise something learned earlier".

(2) ***Drever's:*** "Forgetting means failure at any time to recall an experience when attempting to do so, or to perform an action previously learned".

From the above definition it may be concluded that forgetting is the failure to recall and recognise an idea. It is the weakening of the bond that are formed in learning.

Causes of Forgetting

Why do we forget things? To understand the causes, various attempt have been made and many theories have been put forward to explain the causes of forgetting. Some theoretical and general causes of forgetting are as follows:

(1) ***Forgetting due to interference***: The interference theory of forgetting suggest that forgetting is due to the interference between various information that the memory contains. Interference can be of two types:

(a) *Proactive Interference (forward moving)*: In proactive interference the past learning or old learning interferes with the recall of new learning. For example, if we know English it interferes with the learning of a new language like French or other language similar to English. It is due to proactive interference.

(b) *Retroactive Interference (backward moving)*: Retroactive interference occurs when new learning interferes with the previous or old learning. If we cannot recall the English equivalent of French word that we are currently memorising, then it is retroactive interference.

(2) ***Forgetting due to retrieval failure*:** According to retrieval theory, forgetting can occur at the time of recall, either the retrieval cues are absent or they are inappropriate. Retrieval cues are aids which help us in recovering information stored in the memory. Generally we observed that we are not able to recall a person who we met at a party whose name and face we don't remember. But when someone describes some features of his personality like dress, complexion etc. we are able to recall. The feature of personality of that person acted as a cue that helped us to retrieve the information. Similarly, some time with the help of some cues of learning, we can recall all the learned material.

(3) ***Lack of interest, attention and attitude:*** When there is lack of interest, attention and lack of positive attitude while learning, it is likely to be forgotten easily.

(4) ***Lack of repetition:*** If we do not repeat or practice the learnt material again and again, then there is a tendency to forget that task because bonds are weakened that are formed in learning without practice. It is based on, law of exercise or repetition.

(5) ***Nature of material:*** Meaningful, pleasant, easy and organised task or material can be retained for long time as compared to meaningless, unpleasant, difficult and unorganised task or material.

(6) ***Effect of time:*** Due to passage of time, experiences are forgotten. So, time to time we should revise the learned material.

(7) ***Defective method of learning:*** If the teaching methods used by the teacher are according to the demand of material topic and the student's level like play-way, project, problem solving method etc. then the material learnt by students will be retained for longer time in comparison to some traditional or defective methods.

(8) ***Emotional excitement:*** When the individual is under fear, anger or any other emotional disturbance, he/she is likely to forget easily.

(9) ***Mental disease and mental injury:*** Some mental disorder like psychosis and mental injuries like Amnesia, are causes of forgetfulness.

(10) ***Fatigue:*** Any thing learned while in mental and physical fatigue causes forgetfulness.

(11) ***Long and severe illness:*** Any sort of illness is also a major cause of forgetting. Reason is that all the attention is shifted to being cured from illness.

(12) ***Constant mental tension & conflict:*** Learning in mental tension and conflicting situation leads to forgetting easily.

(13) ***Lack of motivation:*** If the learner is not motivated while learning, (external and internal) forgetting happens easily.

(14) ***Inattentive and rote learning:*** Inattentive and rote learning can be deceptive in nature.

(15) ***Under learning***: It is one of the causes of forgetting which means the amount of material required for learning could not be learned appropriately up to the mark. Quantity of learned material also could not be learned up to the level of a child.

Ebbinghaus's Curve of Forgetting

The studies made by the psychologist Ebbinghaus (1885) present the earliest systematic work in studying the phenomenon of forgetting. He himself worked as a subject for the studies and described his results by sketching a curve of forgetting.

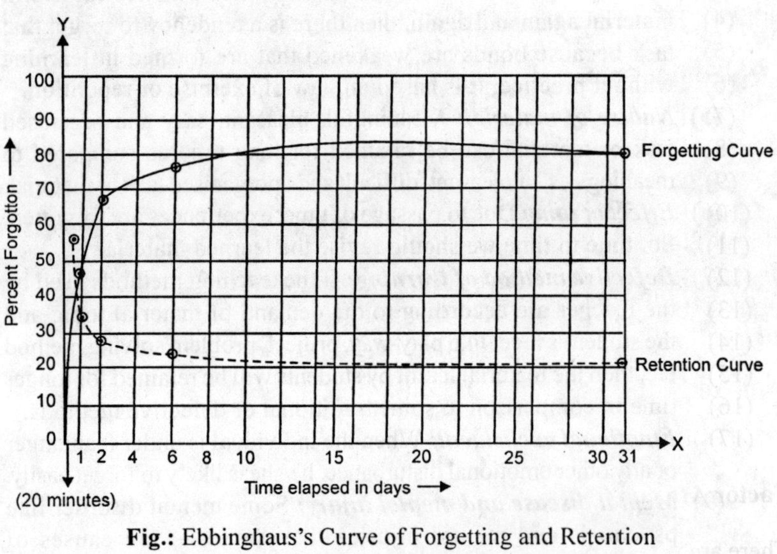

Fig.: Ebbinghaus's Curve of Forgetting and Retention

What he did was memorise a list of his non-sense syllables and then test himself at intervals from 20 minutes to a month to see how much of the list he remembered. The results in terms of the percentage of material forgotten with the lapse of time were found in the following order:

Time elapsed	*Amount forgotten*	*Amount Retained*
20 Minutes	47%	53%
One day	66%	34%
Two days	72%	28%
Six days	75%	25%
Thirty-one days	79%	21%

Ways of Minimising Forgetting

All the ways or methods of improving memory are the ways of minimising forgetting. Here only points are given:

(1) Strong will power of learner.
(2) Taking interest and paying attention in learning.
(3) Linking new knowledge to previous knowledge.
(4) Sound mental and physical health.
(5) Meaningful, organised, interesting and need based subject matter.
(6) Use of progressive method of teaching.
(7) Learning by doing.
(8) Repetition and practice of material.
(9) Formation of clear concept.
(10) Provision of rest.
(11) Providing motivation during teaching-learning process.
(12) Developing positive attitude toward learning.
(13) Using mnemonics devices.
(14) Arranging better learning situation and environment.
(15) Time of learning.
(16) Psychologically sound school time table.
(17) Behaviour, skills and personality of teacher.

Factor Affecting Memory

There are various factors which affect memory. These factors are related to learner, learning material, teacher, and environment.

1. *Personal factors affecting memory.* Personal factors may be divided into two: (i) Psychological (ii) Physiological factors

Factors Affecting Memory

1. Personal factor affecting memory (Psychological Factors)	(1)	Attitude and interest
	(2)	Will to learn
	(3)	Mental health
	(4)	Emotions
	(5)	Attention and interest
	(6)	Motivation
	(7)	Mental fatigue
	(8)	Mental set
	(9)	Purpose & goal
	(10)	Observation and perception
	(11)	Confidence
	(12)	Learning habits
	(13)	Needs (Secondary needs)
	(14)	Physical health
	(15)	Drugs & intoxicants
	(16)	Age of learner
	(17)	Efforts by learner
	(18)	Food & nutrition
2. Content material related factors affecting memory	(1)	Meaningfulness of the content material/task
	(2)	Difficulty level of the content
	(3)	Appropriate length of content
	(4)	Appropriateness of the content
	(5)	Pleasantness of content/task
	(6)	Logical organised content
	(7)	Need based content
3. Teacher related factors affecting memory	(1)	Use of progressive method of teaching
	(2)	Knowledge of content
	(3)	Use of maxims of teaching

(Contd.)

	(4)	Behaviour and personality of teacher
	(5)	Knowledge of child psychology
	(6)	Teacher-pupil relations
	(7)	Proper use of motivational techniques
4. Environmental related factors affecting memory	(1)	Classroom environment
	(2)	Timetable based on psychological principles
	(3)	Healthy home environment
	(4)	Learning activities and active participation
	(5)	Good relationship between parent, teachers and peers
	(6)	Democratic discipline

2.7 TRANSFER OF LEARNING

Learning is a dynamic process. Therefore, whatever we learnt in one situation must be applied in other situation or in future life of learner. Various subjects in school curriculum are included on the basis of their utility or practical value in daily life. For example, we include mathematics subject in the curriculum on the assumption that knowledge of various concepts of mathematics such as addition, subtraction, multiplication, division, fractions, ratio, percentage, profit & loss etc. and many more will be used to solve daily life problems.

Meaning and Definitions of Transfer of Learning

Briefly speaking "transfer of learning is the application or carry over the knowledge, skill, attitude, habits, from one learning situation to another." For example, learning of riding a bicycle is helpful to the learning of riding a bike. Also learning of addition and subtraction is helpful to learn multiplication and division. Therefore, learning or skill acquired in one task is transferred or carried over to other tasks. Transfer of learning occurs when the learner:

- recognises common features among concepts, skills, or principles.
- links the information in memory and sees the value of utilising what was learned in one situation to another.

Some important definitions given by psychologists are:

(1) **Crow and Crow:** "The carryover of habits of thinking, feeling, or working, of knowledge or skills from one learning area to another usually is referred to as transfer of training".

(2) **Kolensik, Walter:** "The application or carryover of knowledge, skills, habits, attitudes or other responses from the situation in which they are initially acquired to some other situation".

(3) **Guthrie and Powers:** "Transfer may be defined as a process of extending and applying behaviour".

In this way we can define that transfer of learning occurs when a person's learning in one situation or task influences his learning and performance in other situation or task. It is the carryover of learning from one situation to other. Also more the understanding, better will be transfer of learning. When we teach other persons those skills or knowledge that we have acquired they also comes under transfer of learning.

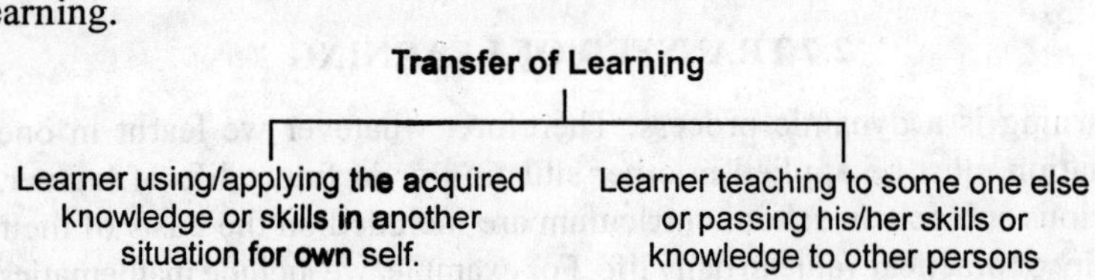

In Transfer of Learning learner uses/applies the acquired knowledge or skills in another situation for own self or teaching to some one else or passing his/her skills or knowledge to other persons

Type of Transfer of Learning

Transfer of learning may be of different types. Some are as follows:

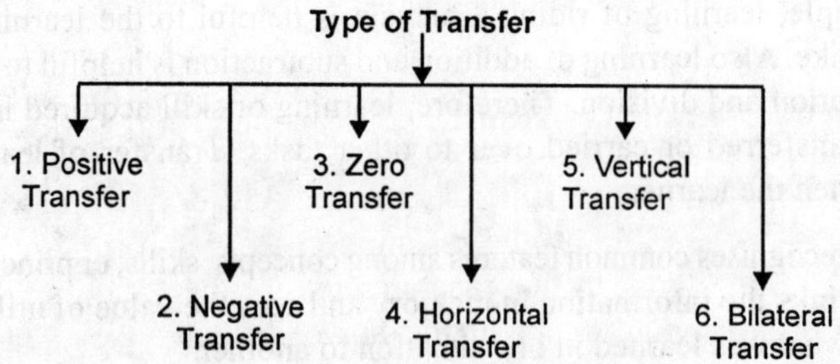

1. **Positive Transfer:** When a learned task facilitates the learning of another task, it is known as positive transfer of learning. When previously learned knowledge or experience benefits the learning in new situations, then transfer is said to be positive. For example, the learning of addition and subtraction facilitates in learning of multiplication and division. Learning the four basic operation of mathematics benefits a person to solve daily life problems related to these operations.

   Learning to construct sentences assists students in writing compositions.
2. **Negative Transfer:** When learning of one task hinders or disrupts the learning of another task, it is known as negative transfer of learning. According to Boring, "When one learning task makes learning a second task harder, it is called negative transfer".

   Learning of driving car on left hand side may hinder to drive a car on right hand side.
3. **Zero Transfer:** When learning in one situation neither benefits or hinders the learning in an other situation, it is called zero transfer. For example riding bicycle and cooking food.
4. **Horizontal transfer:** It is a type of transfer in which learner stays within the same behavioural category in making the transfer.
5. **Vertical Transfer:** Here Aspects of initial skills are used to build more advanced skills. Previous knowledge essentially helps in acquiring new knowledge, e.g. transfer of initial learning to multiplication helps in raising of numbers to power, like squaring, cubing, etc. All this is vertical transfer.
6. **Bilateral Transfer:** When training imparted to one part or lateral (right or left part of body) automatically transfered to another part or lateral ten it is known as bilateral transfer. For example, our training of writing or working with right hand can be transferred to the left hand as well but this process will take some time.

Educational Implication of Transfer of Learning

Transfer of learning occupies important place in the process of education. All education is based upon the assumption that knowledge, skills, attitudes, habits, acquired by the leaner in school are helpful to deal with daily life situations. Educational implication of transfer of learning can be discussed under the following points:

(1) ***Integrated Curriculum:*** To achieve maximum transfer, curriculum should be integrated. For this purpose there should be:

- Correlation among different subjects
- Correlation among school subjects with daily life
- Correlation among different branches of subject
- Correlation of different topics within the same branches

Along with these correlations, curriculum should be meaningful, utility based and interesting.

(2) ***Use of Teaching-Learning Material:*** The basic concepts and fundamental principles of the subject should be taught with the help of activities chart, models, stories, maps, globe and other audio-visual aids. These materials are helpful for better understanding of concepts and create attention and interest of student. Better the understanding, better will be the transfer of learning.

(3) ***Use of innovative methods and approaches of teaching***: Project method, problem solving method, heuristic, constructivist approach, role playing, excursion are some methods and approaches which make the concepts clear to students who can utilise them in new situations as well.

(4) ***Emphasis on correlation:*** Emphasis should be given on correlation. The previous knowledge should be linked with the present learning. Past experience of the learner should be taken in account. Also what is being learned should be properly correlated to daily life and other areas of study. Teacher should provide opportunity to see the similarties and differences between two concepts, phenomenon.

(5) ***Emphasis on learning by doing and learning by insight:*** Rote learning should be avoided. The habit of learning through insight and understanding should be develops so that previous experiences can be used to solve new problems. Also he/she should try to learn through his own efforts. Learners should discuss the things themselves.

(6) ***Emphasis on principles, rules and generalisation:*** For maximum transfer of learning, instead of learning isolated facts, the emphasis should be given on principles, rules and generalisation. Teacher should encourage students to discover the formulas and rules and opportunities should be given to utilise these formulas and rules in other situations.

(7) ***Linking theoretical knowledge acquired in a classroom to***

practical: Students should be encouraged to link theoretical knowledge to daily life. For example if teacher gives the concept of area in class then he/she should ask student to find out the area of different thing available in home.

Factors Affecting Transfer of Learning

Factors which affects the transfer of learning are as follows:

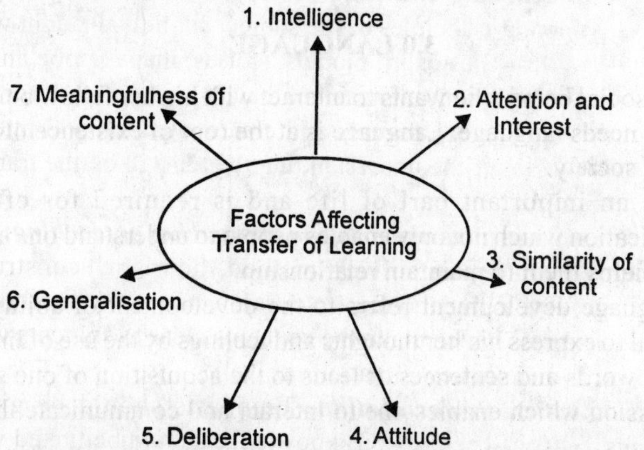

1. ***Intelligence***: Children with high intelligence can transfer their learning more effectively than children of low intelligence.
2. ***Similarity of content:*** If two contents are similar to each other, then transfer of learning will be more.
3. ***Attitude:*** Positive attitude towards learning is essential for transfer of learning with positive attitude he/she can understand the concept properly.
4. ***Attention and interest:*** Attention and interest of learner is very important under psychological factors for transfer of learning. If the learner is attentive and interested in activity, he can learn effectively and transfer it in other situations easily.
5. ***Generalisation:*** Learner uses the previous experiences and knowledge and generalises the facts of transferable situation. Therefore, the learner should make generalisations.
6. ***Deliberation:*** The Learner has to deliberate effort to transfer the learned knowledge.
7. ***Meaningfulness of contents:*** Meaningful contents having more transfer value.

3
Language Learning

3.0 LANGUAGE

Man is a social being who wants to interact with his/her fellow beings for which he needs language. Language is at the root of existence of human beings in society.

It is an important part of life and is required for effective communication which not only enables people to understand one another, but also helps them to maintain relationship.

Language development refers to the development of ability of an individual to express his/her thoughts and feelings by the use of linguistic symbols, words and sentences. It leads to the acquisition of one's power of expression which enables one to interact and communicate thoughts and feelings.

Definitions of Language

According to the **Encyclopaedia Britannica**, "Language is an arbitrary system of vocal symbols by means of which human beings, as members of a social group and participants in culture, interact and communicate."

Allen considers language a means of communicating thoughts and **Feldman** defines it as the communication of information through symbols arranged according to systematic rules.

Hurlock thinks that language encompasses every means of communication in which thoughts and feelings are symbolized so as to convey meaning. It is available in different forms written as well as spoken. Signs and gestures are also used to communicate in a limited way.

Types of Language

Language is of two types: non-verbal and verbal.

1. Non-Verbal Language: It is a type of expression which involves different kinesic expressions. An individual can express his/her feelings through them.

2. Verbal Language: A verbal language involves combinations of sounds which form words and sentences for the expression of ideas and feelings. It is realised by activities like reading, writing, listening and speaking.

Nature of Language

Aspects of the nature of language have been expressed in various ways:

1. *Language is a System*: Language is a system of a complex whole like the human body which has different parts inter-connected with each other and operates in coordination. Language represents a system which involves the coordinated functions of sounds, words and sentence in structures.

2. *Language is Learnt:* Language does not automatically come to an individual. It is acquired by the individual in a society.

3. *Language is Social Artefacts:* Language is rooted in a society and its culture. To acquire it is an inherent potential of individuals. This inherent power is enriched through interaction with fellow beings.

4. *Language is Evolutionary*: Language has developed in the process of the development of human civilization. It is in the process of continuous evolution. Different sounds, words, phrases and sentences are added in the process of human development. Human speech is modified and refined over the years. Man is working continuously to develop and innovative fresh usage of language.

5. *Language is a Dynamic Phenomenon:* Language is not a static but a dynamic phenomenon. It undergoes a process of continuous change. The primitive man's language has been changed, modified and refined to modern languages due to the impact of modern culture and scientific developments.

6. *Language is a Means, not an End:* Language is a means of communication. Man shares his ideas and feelings with his fellow beings either verbally or non-verbally. All literatures are expressions of languages in different forms. Language is communicated for different purposes. It is a means and not an end in itself.

3.1 LANGUAGE ACQUISITION

"Acquisition requires meaningful interaction in the natural communication—in which speakers are concerned not with the form of their utterances but with the messages they are conveying and understanding" (Stephen Krashen).

One acquires a second language through a subconscious process during which one is unaware of grammatical rules. It is similar to the way one acquires first language (native language or mother tongue). Here the emphasis is on acquring the text of communication and not on the theoretical knowledge of its structures. It automatically develops familiarity with the phonetic features of the language as well as its grammatical structures and vocabulary.

3.2 LANGUAGE LEARNING

Language learning is the result of direct instruction of a language. One needs to have one's conscious knowledge. The concept of language learning is linked to the traditional approach to the study of language. Here the main focus is on the understanding of forms, structures, and rules of grammar. Teaching and learning are based on the formal syllabus. Students are taught about various rules and forms of a language with a view to being able to communicate in it.

Role of Early Home Training in Language Acquisition

A child acquires his/her first language in his/her family. By talking to the child the family members help him/her. As a child he/she learns vocabulary—pronunciation and structures from the people he/she meets in his/her neighbourhood. According to various psychologists, literacy in the family helps the learner in getting confidence and in becoming good communicator. Parents can encourage their children to communicate by various means. They can tell them stories or read a book aloud. The initial education imparted by them is considered to be the best motivation for the child to acquire a language. Studies have shown that children who are taught the art of communication during early childhood have good vocabulary and better grammar than those who are not. Some simple linguistic activities that nurture child's language development at an early stage are as follows:

- Talking to the child as much as possible and giving him/her opportunities to respond.
- Using animated gestures, along with words.
- Using proper words with correct pronunciation while addressing the baby by name.
- Commenting on sounds in the environment.
- Talking to the child in simple sentences and asking questions.
- Enjoying music with the child.
- Telling stories to the child.

- Gently repeating correctly words that the child has not pronounced correctly rather than criticizing him/her.
- Talking about ongoing activities.
- Talking about what the child is doing every day.
- Going to zoo, aquarium or children's museum and telling him/her about different objects, persons, names and characteristics.
- Reading good story books with pictures.
- Encouraging the child to acquire new words.

Psychological and Social Factors Affecting Language Development

Factors that affect language development are as follows:

1. Level of Intelligence
2. Physical Health
3. Maturation
4. Motivation
5. Personal Characteristics
6. Socio-economic Status
7. Social Learning Opportunity
8. Home Environment
9. Psychological Disorder
10. Social Fear
11. Good Mental Health
12. Good School Environment

(1) **Level of Intelligence:** Various studies reveal that children with high intelligence or high IQ level talk very early and are advanced in every phase/stage of language development. Children with high I.Q. acquire an enriched vocabulary which children with low IQ do not. They have more ability to construct correct compound and complex sentences than the children with low IQ.

(2) **Physical Health:** Physical health also affects the language development of a child. Prolonged and serious illness during the early years of life can retard the child's language development. Due to illness, the child does not get much opportunity to interact with his/her peer groups which delays his/her language development.

(3) **Maturation:** For proper language development, sense organs should function properly.

(4) **Motivation:** When a child is at the early stage of acquisition of learning, he/she should be motivated to speak correctly.

(5) **Personal Characteristics:** Researches reveal that children who are extrovert and zestful learn language early and more effectively than introvert and shy children.

(6) **Socio-Economic Status:** Children of high socio-economic status have a rich vocabulary and more linguistic ability than those of lower socio-economic status. Children belonging to high economic status have better facilities and means of learning like TV, radio, magazines, computer, internet etc. which help them in using learning skills effectively.

(7) **Opportunities of Social Learning:** Some researches (Bandura, 1967) observe that the child who gets more opportunity of social interactions acquire language more easily than those who do not get it. Children learn through interaction with peer group. While playing, they are affected by language of the peer group.

(8) **Home Environment/Imitation of Language:** Healthy and congenial home environment also influences the language development of children. Opportunity should be given to children to express themselves. The speech of family members and their interest in language, especially reading and conversation influence children's language. The type of family (joint or nuclear) the child belongs to also influences the language development of child. In a joint family a child gets an opportunity to talk to many family members than in a nuclear family.

(9) **Psychological Disorder:** Any Psychological or behavioural problem can limit the child's ability to speak and understand language. A child with a developmental or behavioural disorder (anti-social behaviour or autism) may have limited capabilities to interact with others (Vicky R. Bowden and Greenberg).

(10) **Social Fear:** Social learning or social experience helps the child to learn and understand language. If the child suffers from anxiety disorder or is of shy nature or has social fear, he/she does not interact with other children and adults. Therefore his/her ability to learn and understand language can suffer.

(11) **Good Mental Health:** Mental health plays an important role in proper development of language. Children having any mental illness or disorder face a lot of difficulties in acquiring language.

(12) **Good School Environment:** Education provided in school, medium of instruction, organisation of co-curricular activities (debates, essay writing, extempore speech, skit, slogan writing, poem recitation, etc.), teachers, language competence, news reading, morning addresses in the assembly) library (quality books) also effect language learning of the child.

3.3 LANGUAGE DEVELOPMENT: CONCEPT AND STAGES

Language development is the development of language that supports the child's ability to communicate, i.e. express himself/herself, understand others and developing and maintaining relationship. It also helps in thinking and problem-solving.

Characteristics of Language Development

Language development is characterized as follows:

- Development of the ability to use symbolic expression
- Development of the ability to use words to express feelings and thoughts
- Development of the ability to communicate with others
- Development of the ability to understand expression of others
- Development of the ability to read
- Development of the ability to write
- Development of the ability to speak

Characteristics of Language Development

1. **Semanticity**	2. **Syntax**	3. **Productivity**	4. **Displacement**
It implies understanding the language in which words are used as symbols for objects/ events/ideals	It comprises rules in a language for placing words in order to form sentences.	It denotes the capacity to combine words into sentences.	This means efficient transmission of complex knowledge.

Components of Language Development

Language development in children incorporate the following four components:

1. *Phonology:* Phonology involves the recognition of phonemes and sequence of speech sounds of the individual.
2. *Grammar:* Grammar includes two parts—Syntax and Morphology. Syntax refers to the rules according to which words

are arranged in sentences. The second part, morphology refers to the use of grammatical rules of word formation i.e. inflections indicating tense, mood voice, number and gender, and derivation of words.

3. *Semantics:* Semantics consists of meanings of words, phrases and sentences.
4. *Pragmatics:* Pragmatics refers to rules for the use of appropriate and effective communication skills. It guides the learner by pointing out who says what in which condition.

Stages of Language Development

There are many stages of language development. From birth up to the age of five, an individual's language develops at a very rapid pace. The stages of language development are universal among all human beings. However, the age and the pace at which a child reaches each stage of development differ from child to child. It is generally observed that receptive language development (ability to comprehend language) develops faster than expressive language development (the ability to communicate). Some stages of language development are related to pre-speech form of communication and some stages are related to linguistic development.

Steps of Pre-Linguistic Language Development

(1) ***Crying***: The first sound that the baby produces is the 'birth cry'. Infants cry during the early stage of life to express hunger, fear, pain, disturbance during sleep, etc. As the child grows up and his/her language developes, the frequency of his/her crying decreases.

(2) ***Cooing and Babbling***: Cooing comprises murmuring sounds that the infant makes to draw people's attention. Babbling involves making continuous murmuring sounds.

(3) ***Body movements and gestures***: Infants use body movements and gestures to communicate their needs or desire. For example, a baby turns head away or closes lips, if he/she has had enough food. He/she smiles, when he/she feels happy.

Language Development at Different Stages

Language Development during Infancy (0-5 Years) Stage

Piaget considers this stage as sensory motor and pre-operational stage in view of cognitive and language development of children.

(i) *Cooing*: It begins when the baby is 5-6 week old. Some people think it is vowel-like but traces of cooing produced on sound spectrogram show that it is quite unlike the vowel sounds produced by adults. It is a universal form of earliest speech. It is as natural as the waving of arms and legs by babies.

(ii) *Babbling*: The baby starts *babbling* when it is 5-6 months old. It involves the uttering of vowel and consonant sounds together as in a syllable. At this stage, the baby starts speaking *mama*, *papa*, *dada*, *didi*, etc,. Many people think that babbling is also universal but many do not. It can be safely said that it is sufficiently widespread. It has been noted that babbling in a non-tonal language like English or Hindi is different from babbling in tonal language like Chinese.

(iii) *One Word Utterance*: Between one year and eighteen months the child utters single words. The number of words that children acquire during this period varied between fifteen to fifty.

(iv) *Two Word Utterance*: Between eighteen months and two years, children make two-word utterances. By the time the child is two and half year old, he/she increases his/her vocabulary grammatically and knows several hundred words. Gradually, they start using telegraphic utterances such as *want milk*, *where mummy*, *milk spill*, etc. Expressions such as *I singing*, *black shoes*, *He a doctor* suggest that the child is acquiring some grammatical features as well.

(v) *Short and Simple Sentences*: By the time the child is three years old, he/she starts using short and simple sentences such as

He wants an apple.
I am singing.
He is a doctor.
I help mummy.

It is surprising that guessing words and negative words in sentences appear earlier than the auxiliaries. Thus, *what mummy doing* occurs earlier than *mummy is eating*.

(vi) *Short grammatical sentences*: By this time the child is *three and a half*, he/she starts forming grammatical sentences. Five to eight years of age is the period in which most sentential constructions are acquired. Still their language is different from the language adults use.

vii. *Normal Speech*: By the time children are ten or eleven, they start using normal speech fluently. Their language looks, gradually, like the language of the adult.

Chomsky, who believes in the innateness hypothesis, argues that every child is endowed with rich internal structures of his/her mother tongue which gets activated when he/she is exposed to rich linguistic input. The innate knowledge of structures becomes active only when the child gets "comprehensible input". It does not mean repeated drills of limited structural input, as was previously emphasized by structural linguists and pedagogues. Though language development is added by the input of correctly pronounced words and well organized sentences, it does not depend on drills of sounds and structures. The more a child is exposed to correct data, whether at home, in the neighbourhood or at school, the faster is his/her own linguistic development.

We world like to point out that the psycholinguists of the first half of the twentieth century believed in the behaviourist theory of language development. It meant that the child is dependent on drills and repetition for habit formation. Language development was considered to be the gradual extension of habit formation. Recent research by cognitive psychologists has proved that it is not true. Repeated drill of an expression is not a part of habit formation by the child. Repeated use of an expression in the presence of the child is. But which child indulges in drilling a structure in the pre-schooling stage? None. The fact that the child acquires structures without drills refutes the habit formation hypothesis. Of course, it is necessary that the child lives in an environment in which people use the language which he/she is going to pickup.

Language Development during Childhood (6-12 Years) Stage

Piaget considers this stage as concrete operational stage in view of the cognitive and language development of children. During this stage, sense of hearing plays a crucial role, providing the basis for speech and communication skills. At this stage, children become somewhat capable of using logic and solving problems while dealing with factual stories. Language at this stage is used to refer to specific and concrete facts, not mental concepts. By the age of 6 to 10 years, children acquire syllablic stress patterns which help them to distinguish slight differences between similar words. They appreciate and grasp the multiple meanings of words and use them precisely. They develop the ability to acquire new information from written texts and can explain relationships between words having multiple meanings. During this period, children's writing skill develops. They can write complete sentences on easy and familiar topics and are able to communicate in writing.

Language Development during Adolescence (13-19 Years) Stage

Piaget considers this stage as formal operational period of cognitive and language development of individuals. During adolescence, individuals start using their abstract reasoning. Children at this stage use language to express abstract theoretical concepts such as those found in mathematics, philosophy or logic. At this stage, they are able to comprehend abstract ideas and express them when necessary. They can now write, converse and argue adequately with their fellow beings. Their stock of vocabulary is enormously developed during this period and they can write complex texts applying grammatical rules. They can read and comprehend books and literature.

Language Development during Adulthood (20 Years Onwards) Stage

During this stage, language development of individuals reaches full maturation. They are found perfect in all the linguistic skills like reading, writing, listening and understanding the correct language. Individuals over 20 have the ability to carry abstract and imaginary thinking by understanding and using language and can also frame varied mental concepts. They can define words and sentences. They can read, write and understand complex types of literature. It can be defined as the consolidation period of the language development.

Relationship between Language and Thought

There is a deep relation between language and thought. Maximum activities of our everyday life involves the use of language. We communicate with one another with the help of language. Thought refers to the ability to have ideas and to infer new ideas. Language is a means to encode ideas into signals for the purpose of their retention and communication. Some view that language and thought are two separate identities while others consider that thought is impossible without language. But many psycholinguistics have shown that thought can exist without language. Language is a medium for transporting thought from one person to another. It is a tool for organizing and manipulating our thought.

Egocentric and Inner Speech

Egocentric Speech

Egocentric speech is a type of speech which very young children in the age group of 2-7 practise. 'Egocentric speech' are 'self oriental talks. Children talk to themselves, regardless of some one else listening to them. They generally speak about what they are doing and how. For example, 2-7 years old children often talk to themselves (self talk) when they play with their toys or while doing any work alone.

Various researches have noted that there is a positive relation between this type of speech, task performance and achievements. According to Piaget, egocentric speech develops later into full and effective speech after the child gains cognitive and communication skills. Vygotsky considers egocentric speech a part of normal development of communication, self regulation of behaviour, self guidance, etc. Egocentric speech slows down after seven years. By then children stop talking aloud to themselves.

Various theories and research on egocentric speech recognise the significance of developmental data from children which help us in understanding the process of language development.

Inner Speech

Inner speech is a form of internalized, self directed dialogue. It means talking to oneself. This is the speech used by older children and adults as well. According to Oliver Sacks, it is through inner speech that the child develops concepts and their meanings. While in external speech thought is conveyed by words, in inner speech words do not bring forth thought. Inner speech connotes thinking, to a large extent.

We do not know how much language is involved in inner thought.

3.4 FUNCTIONS OF LANGUAGE IN REAL LIFE AND INSIDE THE CLASSROOM

(In the Context of Different School Subjects and Other Aspects of School Education and Society)

Man is a social animal; he lives in a society. To live he has to communicate with others. Communication needs language, so that ideas and feelings can be shared. Thus language plays a significant role in day to day life.

The functions of the language in the context of daily life in the classroom education and society can be summarized as below:

- **Communicative Function:** Language is used by an individual to communicate his ideas or feelings to others.

- **Interactive function**: In interactive function, language is used by an individual to interact or converse with others in society.
- **Expressive function**: In expressive function, language is used by an individual to express his own ideas and feelings.
- **Informative function**: Human civilization has developed due to the advancement of the informative process. Globalization requires mutual sharing of information universally. Language helps in disseminating information through books, newspapers, magazines; journals and electronic media, such as radio, television and internet.
- **Preservative function**: Man is fortunate to have the divine gift of acquiring and retaining language. The legacy of ancient culture, which began with the beginning of human civilization, is being carried forward in different fields like arts, science, commerce and trade. The past experiences of human society have been converted into human culture. The Development of language has helped man in preserving his culture in various forms.

Functions of Language in Real Life

Language performs a number of functions in our day to day life. Some functions are discussed as under

- **To communicate:** Language helps us to share, exchange and express our ideas, thoughts and feelings to other. Without the proper knowledge of language it is very difficult to communicate. For communication, it is important that one understands the language of others. Even those who cannot talk have sign language to communicate with others. Hence, we can say that language is an important tool of communication.
- **Associated with daily life activities:** Language is very much associated with daily life activities for gaining information and knowledge by reading newspaper, watching TV, listening to radio, etc. To communicate through e-mail, text messages, WhatsApp, voice messages, etc., use of language is essential.
- **Helpful in the development of the child:** Language plays an important role in the overall development of the child, such as social development, cognitive development, emotional development, moral development, etc.

- *Language and social development:* Language has a significant effect on the social development of a child. To be social, it is important that the child interacts and communicates with others. A family is also a mini society. Children first learn to communicate with their family members. As they grow, they start interacting with others in society. Therefore, for proper social development of children, the use of language is necessary.
- *Language and cognitive development:* According to Vygotsky, language is a crucial part of cognitive development. Children's cognitive development depends on the interaction with adults, and their cultural norms and environment.
- *Language and emotional development:* Language performs a great function in emotional development also. In early stages, children express their emotions through a variety of physical activities or expressions like crying, laughing, hitting something or someone, throwing things around, screaming, shouting, etc. The exact cause of these emotions may not be always understood correctly. As they grow and gradually acquire the knowledge of language, they are able to express their different emotions through language. Through exact communication of emotions by the use of proper language, the development of a child can be planned appropriately.
- *Language and moral development:* Moral development is a process in which the child acquires the necessary values from his community and acquires a sense of right and wrong. Language plays an important role in the moral development of the child by *explaining* things related to universal values, moral conduct, structure of values as per their country and society by oral, written or visual means of communication. Various values can be developed in children through moral stories, biographies of ideal persons, audio- and videos-based message on moral values, etc.
- *For preservation, promotion and transmission of cultural and social heritage:* Language plays an important role in preserving, promoting and transmitting social and cultural heritage in written and audio visual forms. It is very helpful for the current and future generation to understand and cherish the rich cultural heritage of any country.

- *To gain knowledge:* In today's modern world, there is explosion of knowledge in all fields. This knowledge can reach the child through print or audio-visual media.
- *To utilize leisure time:* There can be many ways to utilize leisure time. But one of the best ways is reading good literature, i.e. poems, stories, essays, articles, etc. Listening to the ideas of great thinkers is also a good way to utilize leisure time. To contribute to various creative activities is another important step.
- *To maintain relationship:* In this ever-growing world, people are busy and do not have sufficient time to communicate to and maintain their relation with others. To maintain good relation, effective communication is very important, which is possible only through adequate knowledge of language.

3.5 LEARNING LANGUAGE AND LEARNING THROUGH LANGUAGE

Learning language and learning through language, are two different concepts. Learning language means studying and learning different languages such as Hindi, Punjabi, Urdu, English, French, Chinese, etc. Language learning is the result of direct instruction of the rules of language. Here the main focus is on the understanding of structures, rules and grammar of the language.

Learning through language means learning various subjects by using a language as a medium of instruction. Language helps one to understand various concepts in different subjects. Learning in classrooms is primarily accomplished through language. The teacher performs various activities like giving lectures, asking questions, listening to discussions in the classroom, and assigning and evaluating reading and writing tasks.

Students engage in academic tasks through reading, writing, exploring the internet, giving verbal answers to teacher's questions, listening to lectures and presentations, participating in class and instructional peer group discussions, being familiar with written texts and so on. In all these activities, students and teachers use language as a medium for exchange of ideas.

The medium of instruction may be any language, preferably the mother tongue. However, it is observed that if one does not have adequate knowledge of a particular language, which is the medium of instruction, one faces serious problem in learning a subject and understanding its various concepts. For example, it is often seen that when students deal with problems in mathematics, but are not comfortable with the language of medium of instruction, they fail to understand the problem appropriately and are unable to solve it. If students are familiar with the language used as instruction, they are able to understand and solve problems easily. It is true of all subjects. Therefore, it is essential to provide appropriate knowledge of the language of instruction to students. Proficiency in the language is needed to comprehend and analyse the problem and to solve it suitably.

3.6 TEACHER'S INFLUENCE ON CHILD'S LANGUAGE DEVELOPMENT

The language teachers influence the language development of children especially at the pre-school and elementary levels. It is important that their (i.e. competent teachers') form of communication is correct and simple. The following points are important for the language development of children:

1. S/he should speak very clearly.
2. As far as possible in the initial stages, the teachers' talk should be based on solid things or chart, etc.
3. S/he should ask the children to pronounce the words repeatedly.
4. S/he must ensure that his/her form of communication is simple but correct.
4. S/he should repeat words. Repetition strengthens learning.
5. S/he should connect meaning when he/she uses new words.
6. For older children, he/she should provide ample scope to develop listening, speaking, reading and writing skills.
7. S/he should help students develop early readings habits.
8. S/he should organise debates, class discussions and displays, etc.
9. S/he should create environments where language may be used for various purposes.
10. S/he should provide structural and semi-structural contexts to express verbal and non-verbal ideas.
11. S/he should encourage students in their creative efforts.
12. S/he should provide a relaxed environment for free expression of ideas, thoughts and feelings.
14. S/he should not emphasize excessive writing or rote repetition.

4
Guidance and Counselling

GUIDANCE: CONCEPT AND ITS NEED

4.1 MEANING OF GUIDANCE

There is rarely an individual who is capable of managing all his/her affairs without any guidance or assistance. Guidance is required for all in every sphere of life for one reason or the other. Someone needs guidance constantly while another needs it occasionally. Without proper guidance life of a person is directionless. Sometimes persons even with abilities and capacities, develop themselves to the minimum of their capabilities due to lack of proper guidance. Also with the rapid diversification of educational streams, vocations and technological advancement, it is quite impossible for a person to choose the right path or vocation according to their capabilities. Various psychologists defined guidance.

According to **Crow and Crow:** "Guidance is an assistance made available by competent person (qualified and trained) to an individual of any stage of life to help him, direct his life, develop his own point of view, make his own decisions and carry his own burden."

According to **Skinner:** "Guidance is a process of helping young person to learn to adjust to self, to others and to circumstances."

According to **Jones:** "Guidance is assistance given to individuals in making intelligent choices, adjustment and in solving problems."

According to **Secondary Education Commission:** "Guidance involves the difficult of helping the students or public in general to plan their own future wisely in the full light of factors that can be mastered about themselves and about the world in which they are to live and work",

Ruth Strong defines guidance as a "process of helping every individual, through his own efforts, to discover and develop his potentialities for his personal happiness and social usefulness."

In the light of above definitions, we may conclude that guidance can be explained as a process through which a guide or a trained personnel can provide assistance to an individual for making him capable of understanding himself, solving his problem and making his own decision adjustments in different situations. Guidance is meant for the whole child and not confined only to some specific aspects of his personality.

4.2 NATURE OF GUIDANCE

1. Guidance is a process. The main aim of this process is to assist the individual to understand himself by solving his problem and making adjustment in different situations.
2. Guidance process stresses on the complete development of possibilities present in an individual. During this process, a person is aware about his own capacities, abilities, and interest etc.
3. To provide guidance, trained persons, counselors, and psychologists are required, as various techniques and skills are used in guidance process.
4. The scope of guidance is too wide. Guidance can be provided to persons of any age, interest, characteristics, and nature.
5. Guidance is based on individual differences.
6. Guidance helps an individual to adjust with different situations of life.
7. Guidance process is helpful to prepare a person for his future life.
8. Guidance helps an individual to develop to the maximum of his capacity.

4.3 BASIC ASSUMPTION OF GUIDANCE

Guidance is based on the following assumptions:

1. Guidance is a universal need. It is required at any stage of life. Abilities and attitudes are not dependent upon race, colour or sex of any individual.
2. Each individual is different from the others. Each individual is unique and has its own abilities, interest capacities and potentialities.
3. Dignity of individual is supreme. All individuals are worthy of

respect and have dignity, which should be recognized by others.

4. Social attitude, personal attitude, perception of individual are basis on which person behaves or acts.
5. Variation within the individual are significant. Any individual can perform well in some abilities but can lack in others.
6. Guidance is progressive, self-direction but not any prescription.
7. All individuals need freedom to take their own decisions and make their own choices.
8. Individual needs continuous guidance programme from early childhood through adulthood and so on.
9. It is a collective responsibily of home, school and society.

4.4 FUNCTIONS OF GUIDANCE

Aims or Purpose of Guidance

Any guidance programme has three fold functions, namely:

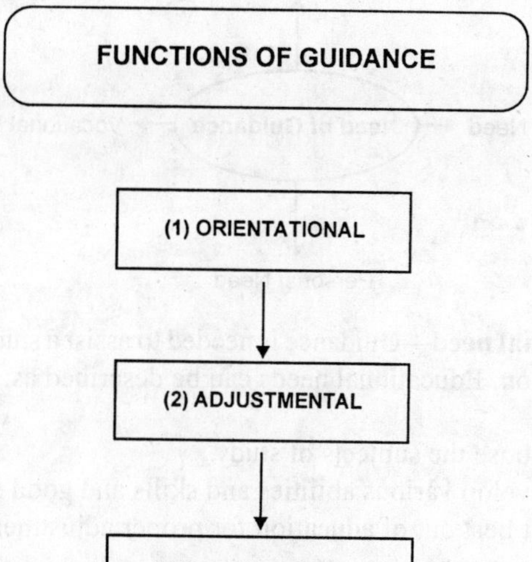

(l) *Orientational aim: The* function of guidance is to orient the children in problems related to career planning, educational programme etc. The experts or professionals provide detailed information to the individual in which they need help.

For examples, if a student wants to choose a particular field for career (like D.El. Ed.), he needs to be provided with the detailed information about that particular course. This is the function of guidance.

(2) *Adjustmental aim:* The next function of guidance is to help the children to make adjustment with the current situation in school, home and in the society. The assistance is given according to the nature (extrovert or introvert) of the child.

(3) *Developmental aim:* Guidance also helps children to achieve self development and self-realisation. It helps them to develop the maximum of their capacities.

4.5 NEED OF GUIDANCE

Guidance is required to all at every stage of life, either constantly or occasionally. Need of guidance can be discussed as under some heads or areas.

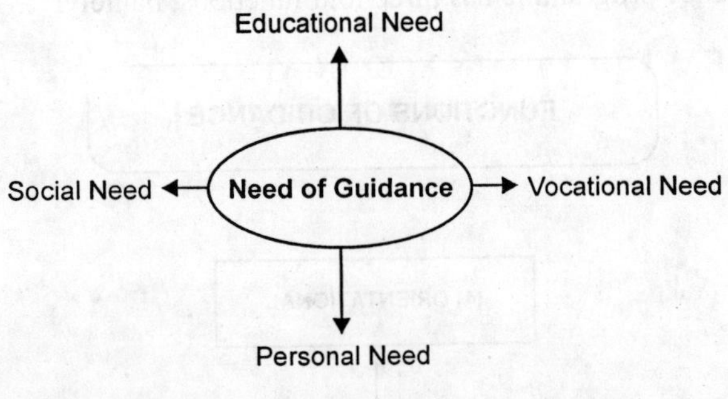

Educational need—Guidance is needed to assist a student regarding his/her education. Educational needs can be described as:

- To choose the subjects of study.
- To develop various abilities and skills and good study habit.
- To get best out of education for proper adjustment with school environment.
- To aware students about their strengths and weaknesses.
- To solve the various problems of education like wastage and stagnation.
- To identify and give guidance to students with special need.
- To sort out the behavioural problems of students such truancy, bullying, lying, stealing, delinquency etc.

Vocational need—Guidance is needed to assist the learner regarding vocational courses:

- Creating an awareness in the child about the different fields of work.
- Choosing a career according to learner's abilities, interest and capacity.
- Providing knowledge of different careers to the students.
- Maximum utilization of human resources.
- Helping students to adjust themselves to specific occupations.

Personal need: Personal needs can be discussed as—

- Overall development of individual.
- Adjustment with self and environment.
- Assessment of one's own strengths and limitations.
- Enabling the individual to face new challenges of life.
- Development of right attitude towards self, society and work.

4.6 AREAS OF GUIDANCE: EDUCATIONAL, VOCATIONAL, PERSONAL AND SOCIAL

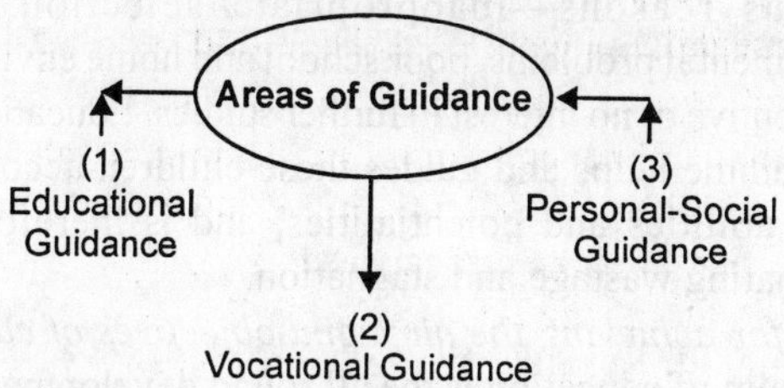

Educational Guidance

Educational Guidance is concerned with every aspect of a student's education. It focuses mainly on the cognitive and scholastic development of a student. Educational guidance is an assistance given to a student regarding selection of school or college, selection of courses and subjects, making satisfactory progress in the school, dealing with examination and adjustment in school etc. It also helps a student to develop his/her potential to the maximum.

Jones defined educational guidance as "the assistance given to the pupils in their choices and adjustments with relation to the schools-curriculum, courses and school life."

Thus, Educational Guidance helps the students in adequate educational development and adjustment.

Need of Educational Guidance

Need of educational guidance may be discussed under the following points:

1. *Need for selection of course or subject:* It is a general observation that sometimes children choose subjects or courses in which they have no interest or ability, and without considering future prospects or vocational implications. They opt for certain subjects because their parents force them or they have no option. When students choose such subjects, it leads to academic frustration and failures. Here, comes the need of guidance. It assists the children to select the subjects or course according to their interest, abilities and future plan.
2. *Need for minimizing wastage and stagnation:* Guidance is needed in school for minimizing wastage and stagnation. Many students fail repeatedly in the same class and drop out due to various reasons—inappropriate selection of subject, adjustmental problems, poor school and home environment, lack of incentive or no interest in further studies. Educational guidance programme helps and guides these children according to their need, abilities and potentialities, and is therefore helpful in eliminating wastage and stagnation.
3. *Need for achieving the aims and objectives of education:* The main aim of education is the all round development of a child's personality. It is possible only through a better educational guidance programme in which all the aspects of the child's personality is taken into consideration.
4. *Need for the solution of various educational problems:* Educational guidance is needed to solve the various educational problems like universal and compulsory education, quality education, high percentage of failure, wastage and stagnation etc. Special guidance is needed for some children with special needs and children with behavioural problems.
5. *Need for proper educational adjustment:* When the child enters in the school he/she need to be adjusted with the educational situations and environmental conditions of the school. He has

also to make adjustment with peer group and teachers. Sometimes child needs proper guidance to make adjustment.

6. *Need for children to get the best out of their education:* Sometimes students have some specific difficulties in various subjects due to which their progress is retarded. By detecting the subject difficulties and providing remedial measures, the overall achievement of students can be improved.
7. *Need for solving problems of indiscipline:* Problems of indiscipline like truancy, students' strikes, agitations, breaking the school and society property, delinquency need proper guidance.
8. *Need for developing good study habits and positive attitude towards studies and school:* Educational guidance is needed to develop good study habits among students and also to excel in academics. Guidance is required to develop positive attitude towards studies and other activities of the school.

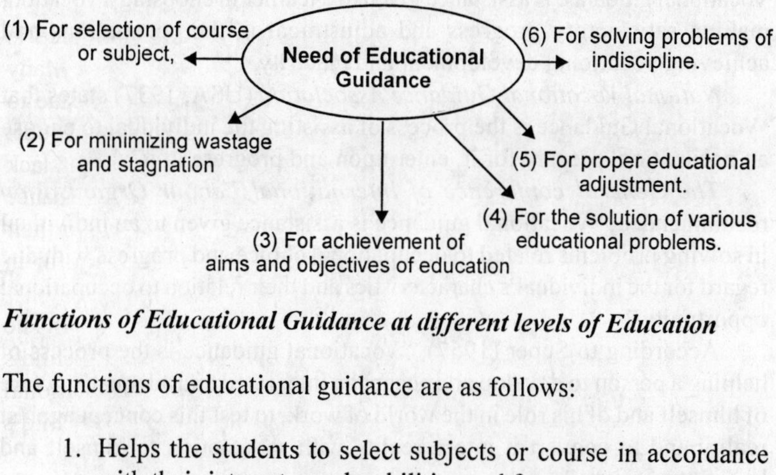

Functions of Educational Guidance at different levels of Education

The functions of educational guidance are as follows:

1. Helps the students to select subjects or course in accordance with their interest, needs, abilities and future perspectives.
2. Assists the students to make adjustment with school, home and society.
3. Encourages the students to know their strengths and weaknesses.
4. Helps in minimizing wastage and stagnation.
5. Orients the students on different courses and its vocational implications.
6. Helps the students to adjust with scholastic and co-scholastic demands of the school.

7. Help Students to develop proper study habits.
8. Helps the teachers to make their instruction effective.
9. Helps students to achieve excellence in learning in accordance with their abilities and interest.
10. Assists students to prepare for higher studies.
11. Helps students to know about the different scholarship and educational facilities/policies provided by the government or other agencies to students
12. Helps the students in self direction, self growth and self expression to solve their day-to-day problems related to study.
13. It assists students to know the goal of education.
14. Helps in identifying, assessing, and guiding children with special needs and behavioural problems.
15. Assists the students to develop positive self esteem.

Vocational Guidance

Vocational guidance is assistance given to a learner in choosing a vocation, making satisfactory progress and adjustment in the occupations and achieving vocational development and maturity.

National Vocational Guidance Association (USA, 1937) states that 'Vocational Guidance is the process of assisting the individual to choose an occupation, prepare for it, enter upon and progress in it".

The General conference of International Labour Organisation recommended, "Vocational guidance is assistance given to an individual in solving problems related to occupational choice and progress with due regard for the individual's characteristics and their relation to occupational opportunity."

According to Super (1957), "Vocational guidance is the process of helping a person to develop and accept an integrated and adequate picture of himself and of his role in the world of work, to test this concept against reality and to convert it into a reality with satisfaction to himself and benefit to society."

To summarize, we can say that vocational guidance is a type of guidance that is concerned with the vocational needs and problems of an individual. It is a process of assisting an individual to get adequate information in relation to the world of work around him/her, make right decisions and choice about regarding occupation, get adequate training and make satisfactory progress and adjustment in occupation.

Need for Vocational Guidance

Vocational Guidance is needed for the following reasons:

1. Need for Disseminating Information regarding Different Occupation

There are many occupations in the world of work. Vocational guidance is needed to aware and orient the students about variety of occupations, characteristics, demands, requirement of occupations.

2. Need for making Right Decision and Choice regarding Occupation

Vocational Guidance helps the individual to make right decision regarding occupation in accordance with ability, interest and aptitude. Wrong choices of occupations may lead to job failure, job dissatisfaction and frustration.

3. Need for Developing Insight in the Individual regarding their Career

An organized programme of vocational guidance is needed to assist the individual to develop insight regarding career. He/she takes decision about career in accordance with the strengths and limitations, interest, ability, aptitude etc. It helps the individual to know himself.

4. Need for Providing Information about the Institutes of Various Occupations

Vocational guidance provides the information about various occupational institutes that gives training to individual for their occupation. It provides information regarding training facilities, entrance exams, placements etc.

5. Need for Making Satisfactory Progress and Adjustment in the Occupation

It helps the individual to make adjustment in the occupation and to attain vocational development and maturity.

6. Need for Stopping Wastage and Mis-utilization of Resources

If an individual selects an occupation in which he/she has no interest and no ability and attitude, then it leads to job dissatisfaction, frustration and all the efforts regarding preparation or training of the individual, becomes useless. Therefore, vocational guidance is needed to assist the individual to select occupation in accordance with his ability, interest and aptitude.

Functions of Vocational Guidance

1. Vocational guidance assists the individual in getting information about the world of work around him. It provide information about the characteristics, functions, duties, requirements, demands, qualifications of the various occupations.
2. It assists the individual in understanding his/her own strengths and limitations regarding the occupation.
3. It helps him/her to make right decisions regarding occupations.
4. It also assists the individual for making adequate preparations for entering into desired profession.
5. It assists individual for making proper vocational adjustment for satisfaction and get success.
6. It is helpful in utilization and development of man power.
7. It is helpful in achieving economic prosperity to the individual as well as to nation.

Personal and Social Guidance

A student faces many personal problems related to himself/herself and his family, friends, teachers etc. Personal guidance helps in physical, emotional, social and moral development. It is also concerned with the enhancement and development of life skills. Apart from personal guidance a student also needs social guidance as he/she meets pupils with different socio-economic status, linguistics and socio-cultural background. So it is very important that the students are trained for developing healthy social relationship.

Some aims and objectives of personal and social guidance are:

(i) To assist the students in developing personal and social competencies.
(ii) To assist the individual in understanding himself/herself.
(iii) To help students to maintain healthy relationship with parents, siblings, handling conflicts related to these groups.
(iv) To assist students build healthy self esteem and self -concept.
(iv) To help students to make proper adjustment at home, school and in life.
(v) To help in maximizing personal and social success in life.
(vi) To help students to develop desirable attitude.
(viii) To help students to develop to their fullest competencies and be good citizens.

4.7 INDIVIDUAL AND GROUP GUIDANCE TECHNIQUES

Group Guidance

Guidance is required by all. Everyone needs guidance from someone from time to time. Although to guide individually is always better and efficient, in some situations group guidance can also serve well. Literally Group guidance means guidance given to a group of students.

To define Group Guidance, **Jones** states that "Group guidance is any group enterprise in which the primary purpose is to assist each individual in the group to solve his problems and to make his adjustments."

View of **Crow and Crow** on Group Guidance: "Guidance in group situations usually is thought of as referring to those guidance services that are made available by school personnel to large or small groups of pupils."

Bennett writes in his book 'Guidance in Group' that "Group Guidance is a relationship in which the guidance workers attempt to assist a number of students to attain self-direction, self knowledge and self realization. It occurs in a setting in which one or more guidance workers encounter students as a group".

Therefore it may be concluded that Group Guidance is a service made available by guidance personnel to a large or small groups of people to solve their common problems.

Objectives of Group Guidance

1. To help people in identifying common problems, analyse them and try to find their solution.
2. To provide opportunities to the people with common problems to interact with each other. This could be benefited by each others ideas, experiences and perspectives.
3. To provide a wide range of information before people for common problem which could be useful for them to find solutions.
4. To identify the cases for which individual guidance is required.
5. To save time, money and other resources which will benefit many people at a time.

Essentials for Group Guidance

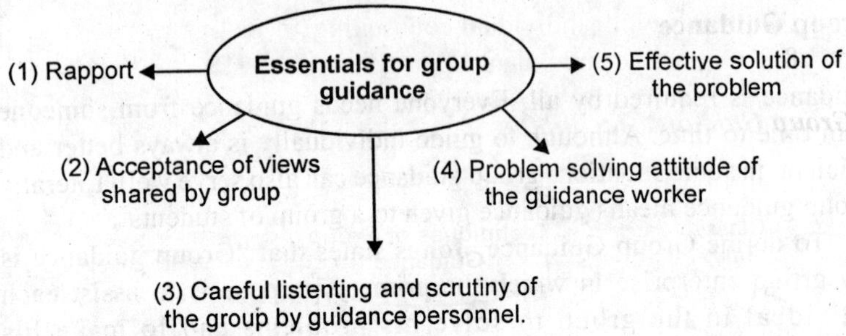

Advantages/Uses of Group Guidance

1. *Economic and efficient:* In group guidance, the guidance worker can provide same information about occupations, courses etc. to a large number of students in a group. So, this technique saves time and energy. The time can be utilized to deal with some other problems of individual students.
2. *Providing unique Environment:* Group guidance offers a unique environment in which an individual learns about and experiences both self and others. A group can provide valuable insight into thought sharing ideas to each other relating to problem.
3. *Avoiding isolation and loneliness:* One of the main objective of group guidance is to avoid the isolation and loneliness. When an individual deals with specific issues or problems he/she may cause isolation and a feeling that he/she is alone in facing his/her problem. This may disturb him/her. But through Group Guidance technique, assembling people with similar issues and problems, the problem of isolation and loneliness can be solved.
4. *Help others and being helped:* It provides opportunity to help others as well as being helped.
5. Helpful to build self confidence and self esteem
6. *It offers students the opportunity to discuss common problems:* Under expert leadership, students within a group can determine what their common problems are? and they can work towards general agreement to solve the problems.
7. *Helpful in the throughout understanding of the students:* It provides opportunity to the guidance worker to observe each student as he/she reacts in group situation and to know some important aspect of his/her personality, unrecognized needs and

problem which can not be revealed in any other way. This helps in the throughout understanding of the student and preparation of a way for individual counselling.

8. Collective and balanced judgment is possible.

Group Guidance Technique

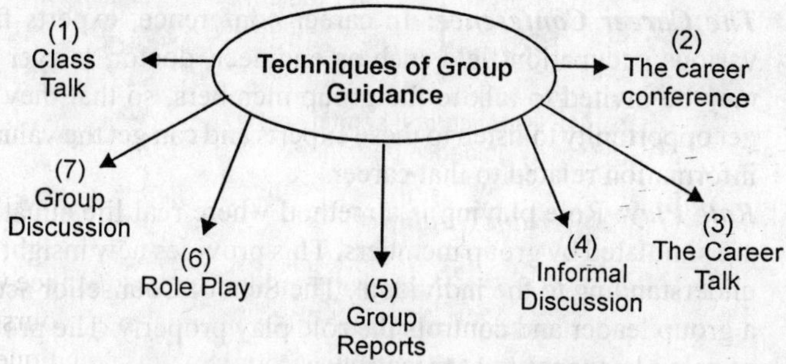

1. ***Class Talk***: The class talk can be arranged by the Counsellor for one class or a smaller group sharing a common problem. The topic of the class talk may be of general nature as effective study habits, preparing for exams etc. It is effective if audio-visual aids are used during class talk.
2. ***Career Talk***: Here, information regarding specific careers are provided to the students. They get information regarding various occupations, demands, requirement, nature of work etc.
3. ***Group Reports***: If the students are divided into groups which have certain specific problems to tackle and asked to write a report and later these reports are presented in larger groups, they can help all the members of the group in gaining awareness of a number of problems and their solutions.
4. ***Group Discussion***: When the group is facing a common problem, then group discussion technique is very useful to solve problems. In group discussion all members of the group interact freely in a democratic manner. The ideas, views and perspectives are shared with each other. The counsellor may act as a group leader to monitor the group discussion. The process of group discussion by experts are:
   (i) Creating awareness of the problem,
   (ii) Understanding the nature and scope of the problems,
   (iii) Hypothesizing possible solution,
   (iv) Explaining the hypothesis mentally.

(v) Testing hypotheses, and

(vi) Accepting the best solution and rejecting the other hypotheses.

For the successful completion of group discussion, it is necessary that all members of the group are conscious of their responsibilities and actively participate to make the discussion healthy and effective.

5. ***The Career Conference***: In career conference, experts from various occupation/field such as engineer, doctor, lawyer etc. may be invited to talk to the group members, so that they can get opportunity to listen to these experts and can get the valuable information related to that career.

6. ***Role Play***: Role playing is a method where real life situations are simulated by group members. This provides new insight and understanding to the individual. The School Counsellor acts as a group leader and controls the role play properly. The process of role play consists of these steps:

(i) selecting a theme (by discussing with students) of play,

(ii) assigning the role,

(iii) assessing the role,

(iv) discussion and feedback, and

(v) re-enactment and replayed if required.

COUNSELLING

4.8 MEANING OF COUNSELLING

Counselling is the central aspect of the whole guidance process. All the activities and services of guidance programme leads to help in counselling process. Counselling is aimed at helping the individual in solving problems and also enhancing personal, social, emotional, educational and vocational development by maintaining rapport. It helps the people to become self sufficient, self dependent and self directed in order to adjust themselves and solve their problems with own efforts.

Several definitions given by different psychologists are as follows:

Merle M. Ohlsen: "Counselling is an accepting, trusting and safe relationship in which clients learn to discuss openly what worries upset them, to define precise behaviour goals, to acquire the essential social skills and to develop the courage and self confidence to implement desired new behaviour".

Roges: "Counselling may be defined as a series of direct contracts with the individual which aims to offer him assistance in changing his attitudes and behaviour".

Perez: "An interactive process conjoining the counsellee who needs assistance and counsellor who is trained and educated to give him/her assistance".

Thus we may conclude that Counselling is a process in which counsellor tries to bring desirable modification and improvement in interest, abilities and attitude of the counselee, aimed to know himself/ herself better and independently solve his/her problems.

4.9 CHARACTERISTICS OF COUNSELLING

1. Counselling is a process which involves at least two persons namely counselee and counselor.
2. The person who seeks assistance is called the counselee and a professionally trained person who provides assistance is called counsellor.
3. It is one to one relationship between the counselee and counsellor and this relationship is based upon mutual trust, acceptance, sharing and understanding.
4. It is more than advice giving. The progress comes through the thinking that a person with a problem does for himself rather than through solution offered by counsellor.
5. It is designed to help the counsellee to solve own problems independently. It makes the person self confident and helps to solve the problems of a person's life independently.
6. It helps an individual or counselee to gain self acceptance, self understanding and self realization.
7. counselling ways for self adjustment by enhancing the abilities and capacities of the counselee for facing the problems and challenges himself.

4.10 DIFFERENCE BETWEEN GUIDANCE AND COUNSELLING

Guidance	*Counselling*
• Guidance has broad area.	• Counselling is a specified service of guidance.
• Guidance can be given by any one who has the knowledge of that field.	• Counselling can be given only by trained and experienced professionals with skills.

(*Contd.*)

Guidance	*Counselling*
• In Guidance, it is not essential to develop high relationship or maintain rapport between guide and the client.	• Counselling demands high rapport building between counsellor and counselee.
• Guidance mostly deals with the problems. That are not severe in nature. Problems related to education and vocation are mostly dealt with in guidance.	• Severe in nature. Also deals with emotional, adjustmental, or other psychological problems.
• Guidance may be given individually or in groups.	• Counselling has to be done purely on individual basis. It treats a unique person in a unique situation.
• Guidance can be given not only with direct contact, but also through TV, Post, E-mail etc.	• Continuous face to face direct interaction is essential for counselling.
• Guidance is not much confidential.	• Maintaining confidence among counsellor and counselee is the need of counselling process.

4.11 TECHNIQUES OF COUNSELLING

Based on the nature of the counselling process and the role of the counsellor, the following are the three types and techniques of counselling:

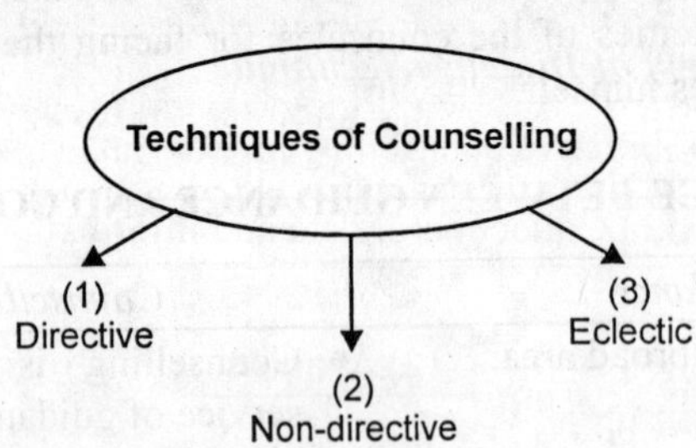

Directive Technique of Counselling

It is also know as **Counselor centred approach**, or Trait and Factor approach.

This technique of counselling is developed by Donald Patterson, E.G. Williamson, C.F. Berdie and others. E.G. Williamson is the chief exponent of this technique.

In directive counselling, the counsellor plays an important and active role. He identifies and diagnosis and provides a solution to the problem of the counselee. Counsellor directs the thinking by infirmity in farming, explaining, interpreting and advising. The counsellor takes decisions on behalf of his/her counselee and plays a vital role in the whole process. Therefore this technique is also known as counsellor centred technique. This technique is useful for the problems related to educational and vocational adjustment.

This approach is also called trait and factor technique as it involves the process of analyzing and identifying personality traits for factors that could best be matched with different kinds of problems.

The Directive counselling mainly works on the assumption that the counsellor is a more capable person regarding training, experience, knowledge than the counselee. He can organize, direct and control the counselling process and can make decisions regarding the problems of the counselee.

Characteristic of Directive Technique of Counselling

1. Counsellor plays an active and vital role in counselling.
2. He directs, organizes and control the process.
3. He collects analyses, synthesises data, diagnoses the problem and makes decision regarding the problem.
4. Central point of the process is the problem of the counsellor.
5. More stress is given on the person's intellectual aspect than emotional aspect.

Procedure (Steps) of Directive Technique

Various steps of directive counselling process are as follows:

(1) Collection of data and information

⇓

(2) Analysis

⇓

(3) Synthesis

⇓

(4) Diagnosis

⇓

(5) Prognosis

⇓

(6) Counselling

⇓

(7) Follow up

The brief description of all these steps are as follows:

1. ***Collection of data/information***: To collect complete data or information about the counselee is the first step of directive counselling. The information about the individual is objectively collected from various records as cumulative record card, anecdotal record, autobiographies interviews, psychological tests, interactions with family members and friends etc. proper attention should be given to reliability and objectivity of data.

2. ***Analysis***: After collection of data about the counselee, it is properly analysed and assessed.

3. ***Synthesis***: At this step, data is summarized and organized to understand the counsellee's strengths, weaknesses, habit adjustment etc. The counsellor should be thoroughly objective in summarized and organized data.

4. ***Diagnosis***: Here, the data is interpreted and the necessary conclusion is drawn regarding the nature and causes of the counselee's problems. Hence diagnosis involves:

(i) identification of problem

(ii) determination of causes that have lead to problem.

5. ***Prognosis***: Under this step, prediction is made about the future development of the problem.

6. ***Counselling***: In this step, treatment is given by the counsellor to the counselee and helped to try different solutions to the problem confronting him.

7. ***Follow up***: It is the last but an important step of directive counselling. An individual may be able to solve the immediate problem through counselling but new problems may occur or the original problem reoccur. Therefore, to help the individual regarding occurrence of new problems and reoccurrence of the original one, and also to check the effectiveness of the counselling process, followup is an essential step.

Advantages of Directive Counselling

Directive counselling possesses many advantages as:

1. It is economical in terms of time and energy.

2. More focus is given on the problem of learner.
3. Emphasis is given to the intellectual aspect rather than emotional.
4. Counsellor can see the counselee more objectively than the counselee himself/herself.

Limitations

1. This techniques is centred around counsellor. It is the Counsellor that directs and controls the whole process. This technique demands more knowledgeable, experienced and trained counsellor.
2. Counsellee is more dependent. He /she is less able to solve the new problem of adjustment.
3. Lack of availability of information or wrong data regarding the counselee can create the possibility of wrong counselling.
4. Emotional problems may be better solved by non-directive techniques.

Non-Directive Techniques of Counselling or Client Centred or Permissive Counselling

Non-directive techniques of counselling is advocated by Carl R. Rogers. In this technique, the counselee (client) plays an active role and all the counselling process revolves around the client. Therefore, this is also known as client centred counselling.

Here, counselee is encouraged to lead conversation and express his/here own feeling, attitudes and ideas. The counsellor establishes rapport with the counselee based on mutual trust, acceptance and understanding. He never interferes with the counselee's ideas, feelings and flow of expression. The client is encouraged and motivated from time to time or as and when needed. He builds an environment that can help the counselee to solve problems and make decisions with his/her own effort. This technique also gives importance to the emotional aspect.

Non directive counselling mainly works on the assumption that individual has sufficient means, abilities, attitude, capacities to solve his/her own problems. Such an environment is provided by the counsellor in which mutual interaction based on trust and understanding can take place and the client can make his/her own decisions regarding problems.

Characteristics of Non-Directive Counselling

1. It is counselee centred technique of counselling. Here counselee plays an active and important role in counselling.

2. It is based on the belief that a person has adequate capacity and ability to make right decision about a problem.
3. Counsellee leads the conversation and act with his/her own intellect.
4. The counsellor remains passive to the maximum. An environment is provided by the counsellor close and constant interaction between counsellor and counselee takes place, and the counselee becomes capable of solving his/her problems with own effort.
5. Counsellor motivates and encourages counselee to express himself/herself freely.
6. Diagnostic instruments are not used in this technique.
7. In this type of counselling, the entire responsibility is shifted to the client or the counselee.
8. The counsellor can quote some examples for the benefit of client.
9. The ultimate decision has to taken by the client.
10. Major aim in this process is to prepare the client to solve problems independently.

Counselling Process of Non-Directive Approach

This process comprises 6+1=7 steps

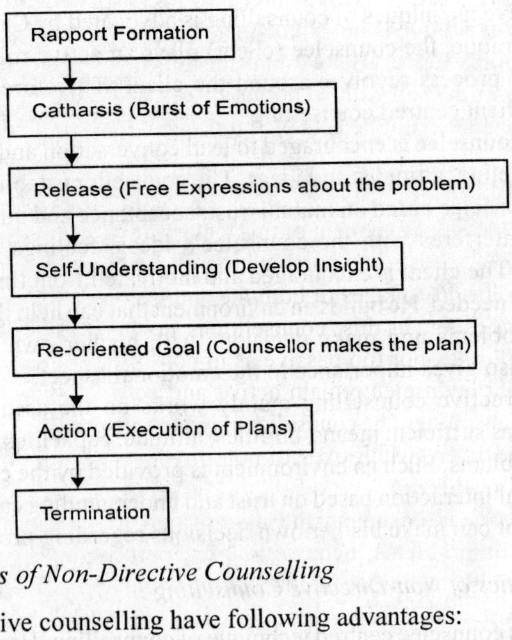

Advantages of Non-Directive Counselling

Non-directive counselling have following advantages:

1. This technique of counselling is client-centred. Therefore full

freedom is given to the counselee to identify his/her own abilities, strengths the weaknesses and capacities to solve the problems with his/her own efforts.

2. Non-directive counselling is helpful in developing problem solving ability, self dependence, self consciousness of the individual.
3. It is very helpful in solving emotional problems and repressed thoughts of the individual. It reduces tension and anxiety due to catharsis.
4. It provides more friendly, co-operative, trustworthy, secure environment to counselee in comparison to directive counselling.
5. The counsellee is more active in this method in comparision to the directive one.
6. The effect of counselling is long lasting.

Limitation of Non-Directive Counselling

Some limitations of non-directive counselling are:

1. Non-directive counselling is slow and time-consuming. It takes lot of time to maintain trustworthy, close rapport for counselling.
2. If the counsellor is immature, and lacks in experience and ability, this technique is not suitable.
3. If proper rapport is not established, the counselee cannot express himself/herself without hesitation. As a consequence, the desired success can not be achieved through counselling.

Eclectic Technique of Counselling

Thorne was the chief exponent of this technique. Eclectic counselling is defined as the synthesis and combination of directive and non-directive counselling. The advantages of both the counselling are incorporated in eclectic counselling. In this, counsellor is neither too active as in the directive technique, nor too passive as in non-directive technique. Both counsellor and counselee remain active and co-operative in the whole process of counselling. The counsellor may start the process with directive technique and later switch over to non-directive technique, as per the situation and *vice-versa.*

This theory is based on the assumption that individuals differ regarding their problems, behavioural and personality characteristics. Therefore a single technique of counselling is not appropriate to achieve the objective of counselling. Also counsellor can have freedom to select the appropriate technique, required according to the situation.

Characteristics of the Eclectic Approach of Counselling

1. This approach is the combination of directive and non-directive approaches.
2. In the initial phase, the counsellor takes up major roles and later, allows the client to think for himself or vice versa.
3. The counsellor has the freedom to use any technique or procedure considered most appropriate.
4. He may use directive techniques to solve the academic area related problems and non-directive techniques for emotional problems.
5. This approach is based upon the logic that a purposeful and reciprocal relationship can exist between two individuals in which a trained counsellor helps the other to change him self or environment.
6. The aim of this approach is to facilitate the process of achieving self-direction.
7. The freedom of choice and expression is open to both the couneslee and the counsellor.

Counselling Process of Eclectic Approach

This process includes the following steps:

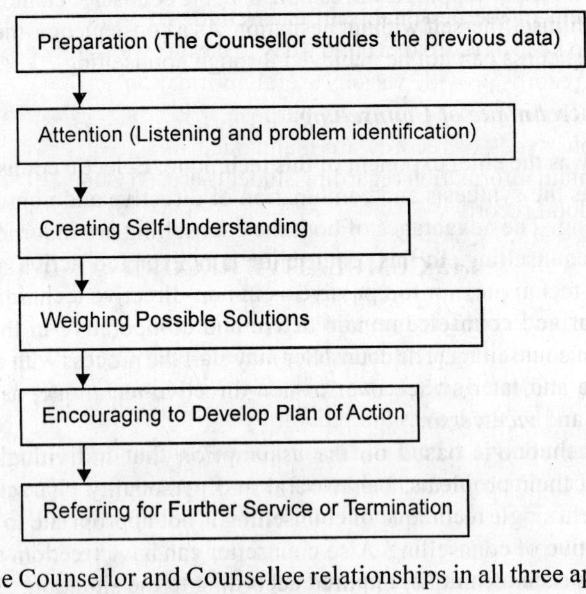

The Counsellor and Counsellee relationships in all three approaches depend upon the following conditions:

1. Acceptance
2. Trust
3. Understanding

Advantages of eclectic counselling

1. In eclectic counselling, both counsellor and counselee remain active and co-operative throughout the process.
2. It is the synthesis and combination of both directive and non-directive counselling.
3. The freedom of choice and expression is opened to both client and the counsellor.
4. There is flexibility in this counselling. The counsellor may begin with the directive and switch over to the non-directive or vice versa as required by the situation.
5. Eclectic can be easily utilized in all the dimensions—educational, vocational and personal.

4.12 MAINTENANCE OF STUDENT'S RECORDS

School is a social institution where children of different socio-economic status, cultural background and diversified abilities and educational background come to study. It is entrusted with the task of an all-round development of the personality of each child. To attain this goal, it is essential to keep a record of a child's day to day growth and development. Student's records provide various useful information and data regarding them, which can be used for many purpose.

Various types of records are maintained in school. Some records which contain information regarding students are: (i) Cumulative record, (ii) Anecdotal record

4.13 CUMULATIVE RECORD

A cumulative record is one which contains the results of different assessments and judgement held from time to time during the course of study of a student. It begins as soon as the child enters in school and continues till he/she leaves the school.

The cumulative record is a record of information about the student which is accumulated from many sources over a period of time. It provides many useful information about the student which can be useful for guidance purpose.

Jones defines it as "…a permanent record of a student which is kept up to date by the school." It is his educational history with information about his school achievement, attendance, health, test scores and similar pertinent data".

Regarding the need for such school record, the **Secondary Education Commission** has stated that "the external examination, singly or together, can not give a correct and complete picture of a pupil's all round progress at any particular stage of his education, yet it is important for us to assess this in order to determine his future course of study or his future vocation. For this purpose system of school records should be maintained for every pupil, indicating the work done by him in the school from day to day, month to month, term to term and year to year. Such a school record will present a clear and continuous statement of the attainments of the child in different intellectual pursuits throughout the successive stages of his education. It will contain a progressive evaluation of development in other directions of less importance, such as growth of his interests, aptitudes, and personality traits, his social adjustments, the practical and social activities in which he takes part. In other words it will give a complete picture".

Hence, cumulative record provides the complete picture as it contains informations about each area of the student's personality.

Characteristics of Good Cumulative Record

1. It is a comprehensive and permanent record of the student.
2. It presents a unified picture about all the aspects of the student's personality.
3. In cumulative record card, information about the individual, kept up to date.
4. Cumulative record card is continuous in the sense that data regarding the student's achievement in scholastic and co-scholastic areas and other areas is obtained and entered from kindergarten to the last class, till he/she leaves the school.
5. It contains reliable, objective, authentic and usable information about the student.
6. Information is collected from the various sources.
7. It focuses on the all round development of the student.

Contents of Cumulative Records or Type of Information Maintained in Cumulative Record

Cumulative record contains information on the following area of a student:

1. ***Personal data***: It includes personal information related to the

student's name, date of birth, father's names, mother's name, address etc.

2. ***Data regarding family background***: It includes socio-economic status of the family, type of family, parents, educational background etc.
3. ***Data of scholastic achievement***: It includes educational history, such as school last attended, past achievements, present achievements study habit, likes and dislikes etc.
4. ***Physical health data***: It includes height, weight, chest identification mark, illness and disability if any.
5. ***Psychological data***: Various informations obtained through psychological tests as intelligence, aptitude, attitude etc. are also included.
6. ***Data regarding personality***: Information regarding personality such as introvert, extrovert, behaviour with teachers, parents, peer group etc. is included.
7. ***Educational and vocational plans:*** educational and vocational plans for the pupil, are also included in the cumulative record.

Along with these, other important and useful information about the student is also included in the cumulative record card.

One typed of format of CRC is given below:

CUMULATIVE RECORD FOR STUDENTS

Name of the School ....

....

....

Address ....

....

1. Personal Data

Name .... Father's Name ....

Date of Birth ....Admission No...............................

Present Address .... Religion ....

Language spoken at home ....

Other languages known ....

2. Family Background

Size of the family .... Position in the family ....

Accommodation: Rented ....

Owned .... No. of rooms ....

Pupil lives with — Facility for study at home ....

Both Parents ....

Father ....

Mother .... Type of family Joint/Nuclear

Places the pupil has lived.

Relationship with the child	*Name and Address*	*Age*	*Education Training*	*Occupation*	*Income*
Father					
Mother					
Guardian					
Sisters Married/Unmarried					
Brothers Married/Unmarried					

Earning members in the family.

	Name	*Relationship*	*Income*
1.			
2.			
3.			
4.			

3. Schools Last Attended

	Name of the School	*Class From*	*Class To*	*Year From*	*Year To*	*Reasons for change over*
1.						
2.						
3.						

4. Scholastic Achievement

S. No.	Year	Class	Subjects (optional only)	Failed/Passed/ Promoted	Positions if any	Name of the Class Teacher
1.						
2.						
3.						
4.						
5.						
6.						
7.						
8.						

5. Health and Physique

			Date	Date	Date	Date	Date	Date
1. Height								
2. Weight								
3. Chest	Normal	Expanded						
4. Eyes	Right	Left						
5. E.N.T.								
6. Lungs								
7. Any major illness in the past								
8. Any disease								
9. Any disability-temporary or permanent								
10. Any other problem								

6. Personality Assessment

1. Introvert/ambivert/extrovert
2. Behaviour with parents: Aggressive/Submissive/Likeable
3. Behaviour with peer group: Leadership/Cooperative/Follows
   Leadership: Always/Somewhat/None
   Sociability: Highly Sociable/Somewhat/Never
   Initiative: Always/Somewhat/Never
4. Behaviour with teachers: Takes suggestions/argumentative/ discusses/passive

5. Personality: Well behaved/Slightly balanced/Emotional
6. Attendance: Very regular/Often regular/Irregular
7. Obedience: Always obedient/Sometimes/Obedient/Rash
8. Responsibility: Highly responsible/Slightly responsible/Irresponsible
9. Industry: Hard working/Average/Careless
10. Home work: Regular/Irregular/Does no home work
11. Self-confidence: Always/Often/Never/Over confident
12. Cooperative: Always/Often/Seldom cooperative
13. Personal appearance: Neatly dressed/Seldom/Never

7. Psychological Test Data

S. No.	*Year*	*Class*	*Name of Tests*	*Scores & Grades*	*Name of the Course*
1.					
2.					
3.					
4.					
5.					
6.					

8. Co-curricular Activities

S. No.	*Year & Class*	*Remarks**
1.	Sports & Games	
2.	Dramatics	
3.	Literary	
4.	Social Service	
5.	Athletics	
6.	N.C.C./A.C.C.	
7.	Any other	

* Mention any special achievement, awards, merit certificates or scholarship etc.

9. Activities Outside School

1. Work Experience in ....
   Part time or full time job ....
2. Hobbies ....

10. Future Planning

1. Educational .... Parents .... Pupil's ....
2. Vocational .... Parents .... Pupil's

The CRC may contain additional information of the following types:

* Correspondence with parents
* Anecdotal Records
* Details of interviews with parents
* Conduct or Discipline.

Source: Guidance and counselling *Vol. I; A Theoretical perspective by Asha Bhatnagar, Nirmala Gupta.*

Source of Information for Cumulative Record

The information in CRC can be obtained from the child or all those who are in close association with him—

- Parents
- Teachers
- Friends and neighbours

Uses or Advantages of Cumulative Record

1. Cumulative record provides systematic and detailed picture of the student along with his/her strengths and weaknesses which helps the counsellor or teacher in proper guidance regarding educational, vocational, social and personal.
2. It assists the teachers and parents in gaining better understanding of the child. It helps them to know the progress of the child in school, his/her strength weaknesses, adjustment, special achievements etc.
3. It is also useful to identify children with special needs such as backwardness, learning disability, physically challenged, behavioural problems etc. It helps them according to their special needs.
4. It also assists the students in gain self understanding.
5. The systematic reliable, objective and authentic information of the cumulative record is useful for follow up and research studies.
6. It helps the teachers and the counsellor to discover special abilities in pupils which should be developed.

7. It is used during meetings with parents about the achievement and school adjustment of their wards.
8. It is also useful in diagnosing learning difficulties in specific areas and planning remedial instructions.

4.14 ANECDOTAL RECORD

Anecdotal record may be defined as: the observed behaviour of a student. It is a record of some significant episode that occurred in the life of the student. It sheds light on the conduct, thinking, skills and capabilities, revealing significant features and characterstics about the student's personality. **(CCE, CBSE, New Delhi)**

American Association of School Administrators 1992 explained: "What a child can do and his or her achievement, as opposed to what he/she cannot do".

Teacher-generated anecdotal records provide an insider's perspective of the child's educational experience **(Baumann Duffy-Hester, 2002 Cochran-Smith Lytle, 1990).**

Therefore, it may be concluded that Anecdotal records are written notes describing events or incidents that occur in a student's life. These are the brief accounts, or descriptions of an incident, episode or event which describe the characteristics, traits of a person in a situation. They are written notes in narrative form. It allows educators to record qualitative information like details about a child's specific behaviour or conversation between two children. These details provide insight about the specific characteristic or behaviour of the child.

Uses of Anecdotal Record

1. It provides a longitudinal qualitative pictures of behavioural changes in student's life.
2. It records minute observation of the particular event or behaviour, any where, any time in the school.
3. It is useful to identify child's attitude, behavioural pattern, interest, peer group relations etc.
4. It provide the qualitative data about the child to the educator and counsellor and is helpful in guiding them accordingly.
5. Many behavioural problems like truancy, aggression, shyness, cheating, withdrawal can be better understood with the help of anecdotal records.

6. It is useful in forwarding a pupil's record, when he/she is transferred from one school to another.
7. Useful in parent-teacher conferences or PTM's while discussing child's behaviour.
8. It assists the teacher to diagnose the specific problem in a student and provide remedial measures accordingly.
9. It is helpful in understanding the child's behaviour in diverse situation.

Cautions during Writing the Anecdotal Records

The following points should be kept in mind while writing the anecdotal record:

1. Anecdotal records are written on facts. Therefore past tense is used to write it.
2. These records supplement other records and should not be considered as substitutes.
3. The language of facts should be 'descriptive'.
4. While observing the event, incident or situation child should be observed objectively and minutely. Also the teacher's personal values, biases, favourable and unfavourable impressions should be avoided during observation and writing notes.
5. Observation should be accurate, reliable, objective and authentic.
6. The student's both favourable and unfavourable behaviour, should be recorded.
7. The record should be regarded as confidential. It should not fall into irresponsible hands.
8. Teacher should avoid general comments.
9. Event should be recorded soon after its occurrence so that accurate and significant details can be included for later interpretation. (CCE, CBSE, Manual).

Format of Anecdotal Record

Name of the School	Class
Name of Pupil observed	Date and Place
Observer	Comment/ Suggestion of Observer
Objective description/ Factual account of incident	

Example of an Anecdotal Record

Name of Pupil: Ram	Class: IV
Observer: EVS teacher	Place: Classroom

Objective Description: When I walked into the class, the students greeted me. All of them were in a joyful mood and did not want to study. I divided them into groups and asked them to play games in groups. Suddenly, I noticed that Ram was studying a science book and was not playing with group members, I became very curious and asked, "why don't you play games with friends?," he replied, 'I don't enjoy playing'. I enjoy reading my science books" (CBSE, CCE manual).

Comment: Ram likes to read science books. He has a scientific temper, but lacks social skills. He does not like to interact with others. He prefers to study science in depth and thinks a lot.

4.15 AGGRESSION

We can observe aggressive behaviour of a person or a child at class room, playground, home, workplace and many other places. Occasionally aggressive behaviour due to provocative situation is common and even normal. However, repeated and frequent aggressive behaviour without any trigger becomes a problem and brings harm to others or and self. Such aggression can cause physical, mental and emotional harm.

Meaning of Aggression

In Psychology, aggression refers to a range of behaviours that can result in both physical and psychological harm to oneself, others or objects in the environment. It is a feeling of anger or antipathy resulting in hostile or violent behaviour and readyness to attack or confront.

Aggression can be expressed in a number of ways, including verbally, physically, mentally and emotionally.

Some Behavioural Activities related to Aggressive Behaviour

- Hitting
- Biting
- pushing
- Fighting
- Using abusive language
- Damaging property

- Threatening and teasing others
- Screaming and shouting
- Misbehaving and disobeying
- Reacting in a bad manner instead of responding
- Beating or hitting self
- Bullying
- Showing anti-social behaviour
- Passive aggressive behaviour and body language

Causes of Aggression

Some probable causes related to aggression may be as follows:

- Ongoing and unrelieved stress
- Family stress, disruption and conflict
- Lack of appropriate problem solving and coping strategies
- Uncongenial home and family environment
- Instability and the lack of a safe and secure environment at work
- Poor parenting
- Illness
- Unsatisfied physiological and socio-psychological needs
- Mass media showing violent and aggressive programmes
- Anti-Social peer group
- Peer pressure
- Substance abuse
- Poor relationship with family members
- Violent and aggressive behaviour of members at home
- Some mental health conditions as Autism Spectrum Disorder, Attention Deficit hyperactivity Disorder (ADHD), etc.
- Frustration due to blocked goals

Effects of Aggression

If aggression is not treated properly it can lead to some serious illness. Some effects of aggression may be

- Anxiety
- Lack of concentration and attention
- Poor communication skills
- Social withdrawal
- Alteration in mental status
- Difficulty in thinking in organized manner
- Poor relationship with peers, family members and others

- Problem in interacting appropriately at workplace, school or in social environments
- Drug and alcohol use and abuse
- Increased risk of injury
- Self-harm
- Suicide or violence
- Depression

Dealing with Aggressive Behaviour

If aggressive behaviour is not dealt with properly and at initial stages, it will cause further aggressive and violent behaviour and can damage the personality. It is important to identify the root causes of such behaviour so that it can be treated properly.

Some of the following suggestions could be helpful in dealing with the aggressive behaviour of children.

1. *No Physical Punishment:* Avoid physical punishment to child. Parents and teachers should understand that physical punishment supresses the aggressive behaviour and is not a permanent remedy. What is required is diagnosis of the problem for appropriate treatment.

2. *Try to Satisfy genuine Needs of Children:* Young children generally behave aggressively when their physiological needs are not fulfilled. So it is important to satisfy their genuine needs.

3. *Proper Use of Reinforcement:* Small steps regarding desired behaviour should be reinforced. There is need to set a limit to aggressive behaviour. The children should be made clear about the desired and expected behaviour from them. If they deviate from expected normal behaviour, they should be dealt with appropriately so that they do not repeat it.

4. *Congenial Home Environment:* The home environment should be healthy. There should be good relationship between all family members. Also the environment should not be authoritarian, controlling and harsh. Children should be able to express themselves freely.

5. *Effective Parenting Style: Parents* should adopt the warm and supporting parenting style. Over protection or under protection of a child should be avoided. As we know children learn from imitation, parents and other family members should never behave in aggressive manner. They should never behave aggressively while responding.

6. *Teach anger management:* Children should be encouraged to express their feelings appropriately and in a civilised way. They should be trained in order to develop appropriate problem solving skills.

7. *Keep an eye on television programmes, video games watched by*

children: It is very important to pay close attention to programmes, video and online games. Set limit to the type of programmes they can watch. The time limit for watching TV and playing video games should be set. The time limit of watching TV and playing video games also needs to be well defined. If possible, programmes should be seen along with the children. Those based on violence should be avoided.

8. *Brief time out*: There is no need to react immediately to a child's aggressive behaviour. It is important to give sometime to the child to calm down. The child can be taken to another room where he/she can be quietly explained about the dire consequences of aggressive behaviour.

9. *Teach appropriate behavioural skills to the child*: It is important to teach the aggressive child how to control negative behaviour. Besides, there is need to inculcate social skills, problem solving skills, conflict resolution skills, etc for the benefit of the child.

10. *Practising some relaxing exercises:* Children with aggressive behaviour should be made to do breathing and relaxing exercises, along with some yogic asanas, which would help them in a great way to remain calm.

11. Children should love physical activity including outdoor games, outing with family.

12. Children should be encouraged to develop some hobbies.

4.16 BULLYING

Bullying is an unwanted, aggressive behaviour among school children that involves a real or perceived power imbalance. The behaviour is repeated, or has the potential to be repeated, over time (Both children who are bullied and who bully others may have serious lasting problems).

Bulling is also defined as a repeated verbal, physical, social or psychological behaviour that is harmful and involves the misuse of power of an individual or group towards one or more persons.

Bullying can happen anywhere: at school, traveling to and from school, in playgrounds, between neighbours, at work place or on the internet (cyber bulling).

Types of Bulling

There are mainly three types of bullying:

(1) Verbal bullying

(2) Social bullying
(3) Physical bullying

(1) *Verbal bullying:* Verbal bullying is saying undesirable things. Verbal bullying includes—

- Teasing
- Taunting
- Name calling
- Threatening to cause harm
- Inappropriate sexual comments etc.

(2) *Social bullying*: It involves hurting someone's reputation or relationship. It includes—

- Telling other children not to be friends with someone.
- Leaving someone out on purpose.
- Spreading rumors about someone.
- Embarrassing someone in public etc.

(3) *Physical bullying:* It involves:

- Hitting
- Kicking
- Pinching
- Pushing
- Spitting
- Breaking someone's things, etc.

Causes of Bullying

Following may be the causes of Bullying:

1. Little affection and openness in family.
2. Defective discipline at home.
3. Poor parental relationship.
4. Aggressive behaviour on the part of parents and siblings.
5. Lack of adult supervision.
6. Feeling powerless in their own lives.
7. Bullies cannot regulate their emotions.

8. Some one else is bullying them.
9. Aggressive personality of bullies.
10. Lack of understanding of other emotions or lack of empathy.
11. Bullies are often jealous or frustrated with the person they are bullying.
12. Looking for attention or increase their popularity or power to get noticed.

Effect of Bullying

Effect of bullying on the person who is bullied may be—

- Low self confidence.
- Sleep disorder.
- Depression and anxiety.
- Frequent crying.
- Poor appetite or digestive problems.
- Lack of concentration in study
- Loss of interest in activities.
- Declined academic achievements.
- Various school problems.

Ways to Stop and Prevent Bullying

Some ways that can be helpful to stop and prevent bullying on the part of parents are as follows:

1. ***Give time to talk and listen to ward***: Parents should give quality time to their ward so that they can share their experiences. Parents should ask them questions about their day school, including experiences of their journey to and from school, lunch, play ground and recess time. Also parents should talk about their peers.
2. ***Be a Good example***: Children learn many habits by imitating their parents. Parents should be role model for their wards. Parents should never express undesirable behaviour in front of their ward.
3. ***Develop good values among children***: Parents should create such an environment at home that helps to develop values like respect, empathy, kindness among children. These values will help the child to stay away from bullying.

4. ***Make aware the child about bullying and its bad effects*:** It is the responsibility of parents to make their ward aware about the meaning and consequences of bullying and its effect in one's life and relationships.
5. ***Pay attention to warning signs*:** Parents should pay attention to unusual signs in their ward's behaviour. This could be avoidance of school and other social situations, change in eating habits and unexplained injuries. Parents should maintain healthy environment in home so that he/she can express their feelings.
6. ***To get appropriate professional help:*** Bullying is a type of behavioural problem. If the problem cannot be solved personally, it is important to take help of professionals such as counsellor, social worker or school psychologist.

Ways to stop or prevent bulling on the part of Principals and teachers

1. Maintain appropriate discipline in school.
2. Make aware students about bullying and its negative effects.
3. Conduct activities which are helpful to inculcate values among students.
4. Take help of school counsellors to solve these problems.
5. Treat students and others with warmth and respect.
6. Teacher should be role model for students.
7. No discrimination among students.

Steps Initiated by Central Board of Secondary Education (CBSE) to Stop Bullying

Some preventive measures are:

1. Constituting an anti-bullying committee with various stakeholders to oversee steps to prevent bullying.
2. Developing training programme for staff, students and parents.

The Board has also recommended 'methods of interventions' for school to prevent bullying. These interventions are:

- Oral and written warning.
- Suspension from attending classes/school for a specified period.
- Withholding or cancelling the results.

- In the rarest of rare case, expulsion from school.
- The Board has also asked all affiliated schools to convene a special assembly to read out the pledge against bullying and abuse in class, assemblies throughout the year.

4.17 SUBSTANCE ABUSE

Substance abuse is a term that is also used for drug abuse which indicates a patterned use of a drug in which the user consumes the substance in amounts or with methods which are harmful to themselves or others. In the long run this behaviour becomes the addictive behaviour. This substance or drug consumption is not for medical purposes. Generally the substance abuse is for mood-altering purposes.

Medline's Medical Encyclopaedia defines drug abuse as "the use of illicit drugs or the abuse of prescription or over-the-counter drugs for purposes other than those for which they are indicated or in a manner or in quantities other than directed.

Some drugs or substances that are used improperly or excessively for mood altering purpose by persons are mentioned below:

Drugs Used for Substance Abuse	*Illegal Drugs/Substance*	*Other substances used for Drug/Substance Abuse*
Any substance which cures diseases or enhances physical or mental well-being is called drug, but when such drug is diverted to improper use then it is called drug or substance abuse.	Drugs such as. Heroin, Cocaine, Marijuana, etc. are taken for non-medical reasons, usually for mind altering effects are called illegal drugs/substance.	The material or substance made for uses in different fields, but are abused or used differently; it is called substance abuse. For example: Boot-polish, Iodex , Ink remover , Thinner etc.

Reasons or Causes of Substance Abuse

Some reasons or causes of substance abuse are:

- Peer pressure
- Mental tension, stress and problems

- excessive pain
- Curiosity
- Boredom
- Low self esteem
- Depression
- Escape from reality
- Inaccurate information about drug effects
- Problems at school or home and in social environment
- Fun
- Self-medication

It should be kept in mind that the adolescence age is most vulnerable time for a child to start drugs other than medical purposes. At this he or she should be taken care of the family and school.

Effects of Substance Abuse

- Lack of concentration
- Poor work performance
- Drug abusers prone to criminal activities
- Fatigue
- Red and puffy eyes
- Lack of interest in activities
- Mood swings
- Desire to stay alone
- Make friends with other addicts
- Lose or gain weight
- Inclined towards violent behaviour
- Addicted to drugs due to long term use
- Causing physical and mental health problems
- Becoming talkative or quiet
- Noticeable change in food habits
- With drawals
- Anxiety and impulsiveness
- Suicidal Tendencies

Identification of Children Involved in Substance Abuse

If a child without any specific reason shows symptoms like lack of interest, fatigue or depression, or any of the above symptoms or sudden change in behaviour, it can be inferred that he or she is developing a drug related problem. It is noteworthy that a sudden change in behaviour or any of the above symptoms could be due to some other reasons as well and the person may not necessarily be a drug abuser but the symptoms should be watched .At the initial stage, parents and others may not be able to detect signs or effects of drug abuse.

Few other signs and symptoms of drug addiction are as follows:

- Lack of interest and carelessness in school activities in which he/she showed interest earlier
- Irritable behaviour
- Aggressiveness
- Occurrences of frequent incidents of stealing at home /classroom
- Negative and worrisome behaviour
- Laziness in all activities
- Lack of concentration and attention
- Decline in academic achievements
- Missing classes and skipping school
- Becoming more selfish
- Changes in eating and sleeping habits
- Deteriorating relationships with family members and friends
- Developing tendency towards lying
- Undesirable/odd objects found in school bags and pockets like cotton, pieces of cloth, silver foil, match box, straws, empty bottles of thinner, etc
- Tendency to avoid old friends, teachers, family members and known persons
- Weakness
- Running eyes and nose
- Change in walking style

Remedial Measures

Here are some strategies for teachers and parents to deal with the problems related to substance abuse.

- Parents and teachers both should engage in dialogue with the affected child about healthy habits and bad effects of drugs on their overall life and body parts, especially the brain. In schools, some skits, discussion, talks, etc by experts should be organised to make students aware about negative effects of drugs.

- TV programmes, movies and video games that glamorize intake of alcohol, drugs and tobacco should be avoided.
- Parents should adopt the warm and supporting parenting style. Over protection and under protection of the child should be avoided. As we know children learn from imitation so parents and other family members should not use these materials.
- Parents and teachers should involve the child in activities like sports, hobby classes, school clubs, etc. These activities usually are positive interactions among the participants which help in developing character and good peer relationships.
- Parents should give quality time to their ward. They should talk to them about their daily routine and give proper guidance whenever necessary. The children should be engaged in different household activities/chores at home. Some specific activities should be planned which involves participation of all the family members.
- The children should be made aware that their parents care for them and should directly feel the expression of love. They should be able to share and seek guidance without any fear or hesitation.
- Parents and teachers should educate the child to understand and differentiate the right from wrong.
- Keep a check that friends and neighbours with whom the child spends time are of high moral values and character.
- Parents and teachers should prepare the children to respond appropriately to someone offering drugs. It is easier to say 'no' when prepared ahead of time.
- Children should be made aware that good and true friends do not influence to do wrong and risky things like taking alcohol, tobacco or drugs. Those friends who insist on taking these substances, should be rejected completely.
- Positive, encouraging and motivating environment in school and class goes a long way in helping the child to stay away from addiction.
- Teachers and parents should keep a close watch on the child's daily routine and behaviour.
- If a child is found to be taking any of the prohibited substances, he should be immediately taken to a trained counsellor or expert.
- As part of ongoing dialogue, parents and teachers should brief the children about the ill effects of tobacco, alcohol and drug abuse. Instilling the right values from the very beginning will certainly help children to keep away from undesired activities.

- Efforts should be made to identify the real cause of drug abuse and to tackle it
- There are certain medicines that are prescribed to deal with drug problems. Doctors should be consulted when needed or the child should be sent for counselling or rehabilitation.

4.18 DELINQUENCY

Meaning and Definition of Delinquency

Every society establishes some social and moral norms for its members to maintain peace and harmony in the society. It is expected from the members of the society to strictly follow these norms. However, there are some persons in the society who violate these established norms and behave in anti-social manner. This type of behaviour is referred to as 'anti social behaviour' and such persons are called 'Delinquents'. This anti-social behaviour involves cheating, stealing, kidnapping, murder, damaging public property, etc. Not only adults and grown ups but even some children suffer from such behaviour. These children and adolescents are called 'Juvenile Delinquents'. The problem of delinquency is a serious concern to all who face this problem as teachers, parents, school authorities and others.

Some educationist have defined the term 'delinquency' as:

C. Burt: "A person is regarded as technically delinquent when his anti-social tendencies appear so grave that he becomes or ought to become the subject of official action."

Good: "Juvenile delinquent is any child whose conduct deviates sufficiently from normal social usage that it may be labelled antisocial".

Richard, A. Cloward: " The delinquent act is a behaviour that violates norms of the society, and when officially known, it evokes a judgment by agents of criminal justice that such norms have been violated".

Causes of Delinquency

There are different views regarding the causes of delinquency. One view believes that heredity, intelligence, physiological factors are responsible for delinquency and the other view emphasises on environmental factors.

Hereditary and Intelligence

Psychologists have conducted many surveys and researches to relate the causes of delinquency to heredity. However, other researches concluded that delinquency is not inherited.

Similarly, some psychologists like Healy and Bronner tried to show relationship between intelligence and delinquency and reported that 37% of delinquents were in sub-normal range of intelligence. They concluded that delinquency was 5 to 10 times more likely to occur among the mentally handicapped than among the normal group (S.S. Chauhan).

Contrary to this, John Slawson conducted a study to find the relation between intelligency and delinquency and concluded that 'no relation between IQ, offense charged'.

So, low intelligence is not the sole cause of delinquency. In many cases delinquents are leaders of gangs and they have high IQ level.

Environmental Factors

It includes the following factors.

Environmental Factors

Home

(i) Broken home
(ii) Poverty and economic difficulties in family
(iii) Lack of affection
(iv) Defective discipline or autocratic discipline
(v) Partiality of parents
(vi) Delinquent and criminal behaviour of parents and other family members
(vii) Immoral parents
(viii) Unemployment
(ix) Over crowded family
(x) Locality of Home
(xi) Domestic violence
(xii) Low socio-economic status
(xiii) Lack of quality time on the part of parents or no time for children

School

(i) Defective discipline
(ii) Improper method of teaching
(iii) unsympathetic and harsh attitude of teachers and authority of schools
(iv) Lack of co-curricular activities and moral education
(v) Difficult course
(vi) Frustrated and maladjusted teachers
(vii) Over-crowded class
(viii) Lot of home-work
(ix) Partiality by teachers and school authorities
(x) Failure or backwardness
(xi) School locality
(xii) Lack of facilities
(xiv) Lack of proper guidance
(xv) Lack of understanding of need of children

Society or neighbourhood

(i) Delinquent and maladjusted peer group
(ii) Anti-social behaviour of society members
(iii) Lack of respect among members
(iv) Inadequate facilities for children such as park

Remedial Measures

Remedial measures that can be adopted **by parents** to prevent delinquency:

(1) Sympathetic and affectionated attitude of parents.
(2) Congenial and healthy home environment.
(3) Democratic discipline.
(4) No over protection and under protection.
(5) Understanding the need and feeling of children.
(6) Watch on the peer group of child.
(7) Adequate facilities at home.
(8) Providing quality time/spend time with children.
(9) Providing models.
(10) No liberal pocket money.
(11) Behaving in a proper manner.
(12) No partiality among children.

Remedial measures that can be adopted **by school**:

(1) Child-centred education.
(2) Use of innovative and interesting method of teaching.
(3) Diversified curriculum according to the need, interest of students.
(4) Sympathetic behaviour of teacher and school authorities.
(5) Experienced, trained and efficient teachers.
(6) Appropriate class size.
(7) Appropriate and adequate facilities for students like play ground, canteen, library etc.
(8) Providing proper guidance to students and parents.
(9) Impartial attitude of teachers.
(10) Proper arrangement of co-curricular activities.
(11) Undesirable behaviour of students to be watched and corrected properly.
(12) Democratic discipline of school.
(13) Congenial and healthy environment of school.
(14) Organisation of parent-teacher meeting time to time.

4.19 TRUANCY

Truancy is a serious problem of education. It is an intentional unauthorized absence from compulsory schooling. It is unapproved absence from school, usually without parents' knowledge.

According to the Oxford dictionary, it means a pupil who stays away from school without leave and explanation. Most experts believes that truancy is a powerful and accurate predictor of involvement in crime, drug abuse and violence.

Causes of Truancy

The causes of truancy underlies within the factors related to (i) home (ii) school (iii) person and society.

Factors/Causes of Truancy related to Home Environment

(1) Illiteracy of parents.
(2) Lack of affection.
(3) Bad relationship between parents and child.
(4) Lack of time on the part of parents to help or guide students in study.
(5) Over protection or under protection.
(6) Involvement of child in other household activities.
(7) Lack of supervision.
(8) Drug and alcohol abuse by parent and /or student

Factors related to School Environment

(1) Unsympathetic and harsh attitude of teachers.
(2) Poor teaching method.
(3) Impartial behavioural of teacher.
(4) Difficult and uninteresting curriculum.
(5) Defective discipline of school.
(6) Bad company or peer group pressure.
(7) Lack of co-curricular activities and facilities.
(8) No understanding about the need of students.
(9) Lot of home assignments.
(10) Lack of interest in school activities.
(11) Difficult content/curriculum.
(12) Fear of violence on the way to school or in school.
(13) Alienation from authority.

(14) Performing badly in school academics.
(15) Boredom.
(16) Lack of academic skills.

Besides, some other causes of truancy may be:

- Low level of physical and mental abilities.
- Poor physical and mental health.
- Social and emotional maladjustment.
- Low self esteem

Remedial Measures for Truancy

Remedial measures for truancy which can be adopted by parents and school authorities are as follows:

Remedial measure that can be adopted by the school:

(1) Appropriate behaviour of the teacher
(2) Innovative and child-centred method of teaching, such as activity method, play way method, constructive approach, role play etc.
(3) Constructive and self imposed discipline.
(4) Proper arrangement of co-curricular activities and facilities.
(5) Proper guidance and counselling.
(6) Congenial environment in school.
(7) Reforms in curriculum. It should be according to need, interest and ability.
(8) Developing good study habits among children.
(9) Co-operation of teachers with parents.

Remedial measures that can be adopted by parents.

(1) Proper care of physical and mental health of children.
(2) Congenial home environment.
(3) Providing adequate time to children for their problem and study.
(4) Providing affection, safety and emotional security to reduce tension, anxiety and stress.
(5) Proper care to satisfy basic needs of children.
(6) Co-operation of parents with teachers and school authorities.
(7) Watch on the peer group of children.

ESTABLISHMENT OF MINIMUM GUIDANCE SERVICES AT ELEMENTARY LEVEL WITH THE INVOLVEMENT OF PARENTS AND COMMUNITY

4.20 GUIDANCE SERVICES IN SCHOOL

Guidance is an integral part of education. To make satisfactory progress in a desired direction, a student needs guidance from time to time. Guidance services are the important and integral part of school programme. **Froelich** defines 'guidance services' as services which are designed to "help the school to adjust the pupil and help the pupil make adjustment to school and life." These services help the individual to become aware of their potentialities and abilities and utilize them in such a way so that he/she can make proper adjustment with environment and solve the problem of life independently."

Objectives of Guidance Services at Elementary Stage

The main objectives of Guidance services at elementary stage are as follows:

1. Smooth transition from home to school.
2. Help potential drop outs to stay in school.
3. Identify and assist children with special need.
4. Identify deficits in basic learning skills.
5. Help students to develop positive self concept and healthy peer relationships.
6. Improve pupil-teacher relationship.
7. Identify and assist students with behavioural problems.
8. Develop healthy attitude towards all kinds of socially useful work among students.
9. Assist students in developing good work habit.
10. Assist in improving academic performance.
11. Assist students in developing critical thinking and problem solving skills.
12. Make students aware about world of work.
13. Help students to understand self in relation to world of work.
14. Assist students to enhance personal-social development.

15. Help students to accept physiological physical changes as they grow in age.

Source: A developmental framework for Guidance and counselling programme in school NCERT.

Minimum Guidance Services in School

A programme of guidance must have certain services which are essential to any guidance programme. These various services in guidance programme are as follows:

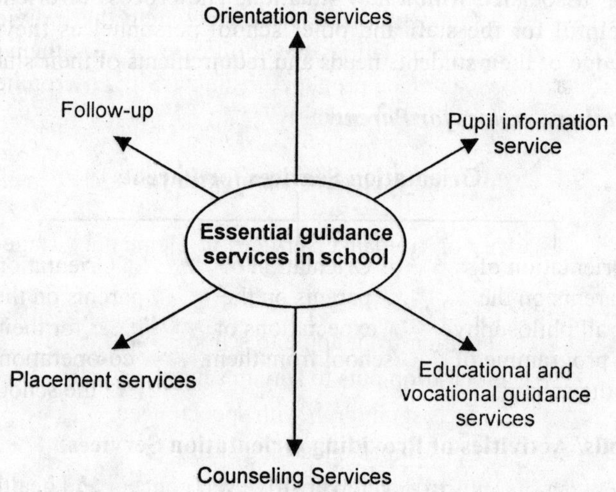

Some guidance services which can be established or organized at elementary level are discussed here:

(I) *Orientation Services:* The assistance which is given to students to help them adjust to the new school is called 'Orientation'. The main objective of orientation service is smooth transition of student from home to school.

These orientational services include—

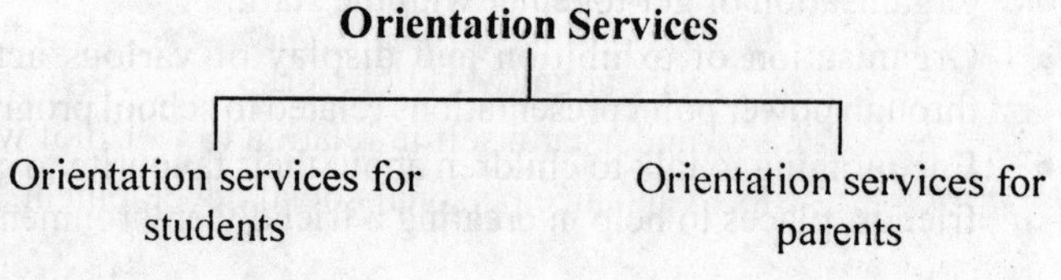

Orientation Services for Students:

- Orientation of students on overall school environment.
- Orientation of students on rules and regulation.
- Orientation of students on physical facilities and equipment available in school.
- Orientation of students on curricular and co-curricular activities of school.
- Orientation of students on the tradition of school

All these orientations help the new students to overcome the anxiety and fear associated with a new situation. The process of orientation is also helpful for the staff and other school personnel as they get the knowledge of their students needs and requirements of their students.

Orientation Services for Parents

Orientation Services for Parents

- Orientation of parents on the overall philosophy and programme of the school.
- Orientation of parents on the expectations of school from them.
- Orientation of parents on the need for their co-operation with the school.

Methods/ Activities of Providing Orientation Services

The following methods or activities may be organized by the guidance worker.

- Meeting and conferences with parents to orient them about the philosophy and programmes of school.
- A brochure about the school, including establishment, overall school programme, pictures of various school activities, rules and regulation, fees, attendance, vacations etc. could be distributed to parents.
- Organisation of get-together with the staff.
- Organisation of exhibition and display of various activities through power point presentations related to school programme.
- Encouraging to talk to children about their favourite toys, pets, friends, places to help in creating a friendly environment.

- Organising various activities as skits, poem recitation, recreational games and to enable children to express their emotions and feelings and share them with others to get familiar with each other.

Advantages of Orientation Services

1. Helpful in getting admission in new school.
2. Assists students in making adjustments with their teachers, classmates and other schoolmates.
3. Helps students and parents to know about the overall school policies and programmes, curricular and co-curricular activities, physical and instructional facilities etc.
4. Helpful in understanding history and traditions of the school.
5. Explains the overall school environment.
6. Provides information about various facilities available in school.

(2) *Pupil Information Service:* The main aim of guidance is to develop students' potentialities to the optimum. To fulfill this objectives it is the responsibility of the guidance worker to maintain full record of each student, such as background, qualifications, interests, habits, achievement, personality traits etc. The information should be updated as and when required. This type of data is useful for readily understanding of individual for planning various guidance activities, organizing counselling etc.

For organizing these informations in a systematic manner, a 'cumulative record card' may be maintained for each student. Cumulative record card is a record of information about the student which is accumulated from many sources over a period of time. These can be used in discussion with parents and teachers, for identifying the needs of the student and providing various guidance from time to time.

The complete Proforma, sources of data, maintenance of CRC, advantage / use are given in the topic "Maintenance of Students Record", Unit 3.

(3) *Counselling Services*: Counselling service is considered as the most important guidance service. All the other services are only complementary to or serve as supporting devices for counselling service. It provide one-to-one relationship between the counsellor and counsellee and this relationship is based upon mutual trust, acceptance, sharing and understanding. Counselling services are for those who are generally:

- Under achievers

- Declined academic performance
- Special need children
- Having adjustmental problem in new setting with teachers and classmates
- Dropouts from schools.
- Showing behavioural problem as bullying, truancy, aggression, drug addiction etc.
- Absentees

In all these situations, a trained and skillful counsellor can provide an encouraging and motivating environment and maintain close and continuous interaction with the client (counsellee). It helps the individual to change his/her attitude and behaviour and gain self acceptance, self understanding to solve his/her problems independently.

As counselling is a highly specialized activity it requires those who are especially trained for it. Hence, only professionally trained counsellors should be appointed.

(4) *Educational and Vocational Guidance Services:* Educational guidance services assist the students regarding selection of school or college, selection of courses and subjects for making satisfactory progress in school in accordance with the abilities and capacities and also making adjustment with the environment.

Vocational guidance services provide information and assist students in choosing their vocation according to their interest and abilities and for making satisfactory progress and adjustment in the occupation.

At elementary level, the main objectives of educational and vocational guidance services are as follows:

- Helps students to develop good study habits for academic success.
- Assist students to develop positive attitudes towards studies and school.
- Identify the children with special needs.
- Identify the behavioural problems among students as lying, bullying, truancy etc.
- Identify deficits in basic learning skills.
- Prevent drop out.
- Assist students to adjust with school environment.
- Solve the problem of indiscipline.
- Develop a positive self concept.
- Provide information and develop positive attitude towards various kinds of work among students.

- Help students to learn and develop good work habit.
- Acquaint students about need and importance of career.
- Make students aware about world of work.
- Spread awareness among students about various subjects of study and their relevance to occupation.
- To develop understanding of self in relation to world of work.

ACTIVITIES/ METHODOLOGY TO PROVIDE EDUCATIONAL AND VOCATIONAL GUIDANCE SERVICES OR ACTIVITIES TO FULFILL THE OBJECTIVES OF EDUCATIONAL AND VOCATIONAL GUIDANCE SERVICES

	Activities or Methodology
(i) To prevent drop out	Students should be motivated to participate in all activities, and after identifying the cause of dropout, remedial measures can be adopted.
(ii) To identify and assisting children with special needs.	Psychological testing, observation, contact with parents, counselling etc.
(iii) To develop good study habits for academic skills.	Class talk/ discussion.
(iv) To identify and assist the students with behavioural problems.	Observation, psychological test, role play counselling.
(v) To identify deficit in basic learning skills.	Observation, diagnostic testing, remedial measures.
(vi) To provide information and develop positive attitude towards various types of occupations	Career information, display of charts or model on different occupations, films on various occupations and discussion.

4.21 ROLE OF COUNSELLOR IN ESTABLISHING GUIDANCE SERVICES

The counsellor is the centre of the school guidance programme. He/she has to work with children, parents, teachers and community members. Regarding the role of a counsellor, **Ruth-strang** has stated: 'The counsellor is like a gardener who prepares the soil and does everything he can do to help each plant grow in its own best way'. The role of counsellor in guidance programme can be discussed under the following heads:

Role of Counsellor with Parents and Community

1. To explain the guidance point of views to parents and community.
2. To give information to parents about their ward's progress, achievements, difficulties in any educational and personal adjustment.
3. To collect relevant information about the children from their parents.
4. To coordinate from time to time with the other agencies of the community as hospital, employment exchange etc. which the students may need to approach from time to time.
5. To keep regular contacts with parents of special need children.
6. To give information about the various guidance services available in school.

Role of Counsellor with Teacher

1. To organize guidance services in school with co-operation of teacher.
2. To collect relevant information for the teachers about child performance, achievements and difficulties regarding subject and classroom adjustment.
3. To collect information regarding the behavioural problems of students.
4. To provide information to the teacher about students' weaknesses and strengths.
5. To help the teacher to maintain healthy pupil teacher relationship.

Role of Counsellor with Students

1. To orient students about the overall school programme, policies, facilities, curricular and co-curricular activities for smooth transition from home to school and from secondary classes to higher classes.
2. To collect relevant information from the students about their educational plans career choices or any other problems or difficulties they face.
3. To orient students about various course of studies, occupations.

4. To assist students to choose right occupation according to their abilities and interest.
5. To assist students in their placement in course and occupation.
6. To provide counselling to students who need it.
7. To assist students to recognize their strengths and weaknesses.
8. To assist the children with special needs.
9. To help the students to develop a positive self concept and healthy peer relationship.
10. To establish rapport with students.
11. To help to develop good student habits, skills, communication and positive attitude towards study.

Apart from these roles, some other roles of counsellor are as follows:

- To organize guidance exhibitions, career talks, career conferences, parent's day, group activities etc..
- To maintain cumulative record card and other records of students.
- To inform the Principal about the progress, achievement of students and difficulties faced in organizing guidance programme in school.

Characteristics of a Good Counsellor

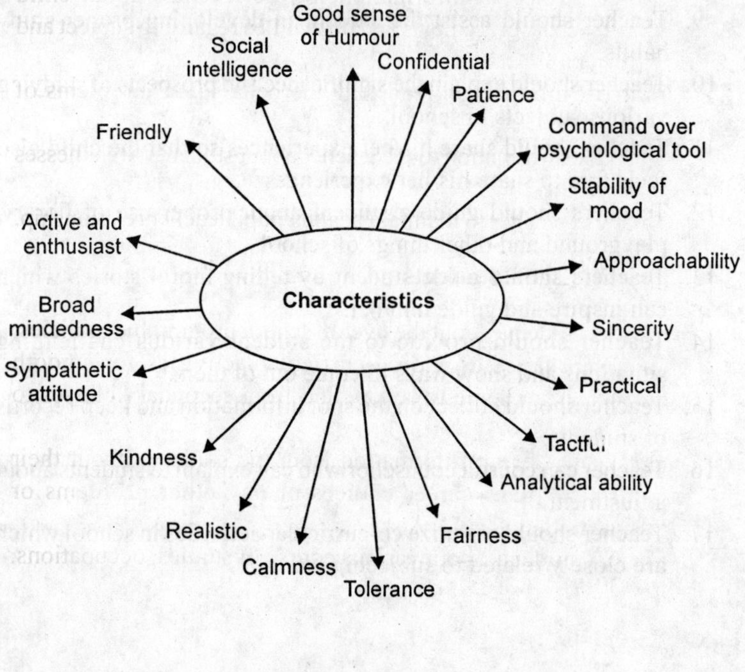

Role of Teacher in Guidance

1. It is the responsibility of the teacher to see whether every child is doing well in his/her academic classes and whether he/she is grasping what is done in the class, and it is the responsibility of the teacher to guide them.
2. It is the responsibility of teacher to know about the child's abilities of reading, writing etc and his/her limitations or weaknesses.
3. Teacher should see the past academic work of child and accordingly guide and show path to the child
4. Teacher should also guide parents for seeing home situations so that child excel in all the fields.
5. Teacher should take weekly tests so that the child does not lag behind in his/her studies and point out the mistakes for improvement.
6. Teacher should know about the educational goals of the child and show the effective way of reaching those goals easily.
7. Teacher should guide the child in his/her personal matter and should see that the child does not indulge in anti-social activities or take drugs.
8. Teacher should know the social circle of the student, his/her friends so he can guide him/her.
9. Teacher should assist the student in developing proper study habits.
10. Teacher should explain the significance and prospects of studying various subjects in school.
11. Teacher should share his/her experiences so that the child also feels free to share his/her experiences.
12. Teachers should guide a student about proper use of library, playground and other things of school.
13. Teachers should guide student by telling moral stories which can inspire and guide him/her.
14. Teacher should provide to the student various challenging situations and show ways to come out of them.
15. Teacher should collect on the spot information and keep records of students.
16. Teacher can consult counsellor who can explain to students about adjustment.
17. Teacher should organize co-curricular activities in school which are closely related to subject matter.

5
Inclusive Education

5.0 HISTORY OF SPECIAL SCHOOLS

One of the first special schools in the world was in Paris, the Institut National des Jeunes Aveugles (1784) . It taught blind students. The first school for the deaf was established in U.K. in 1760 in Edinburgh by Thomas Braidwood, with education for visually impaired people.

In the 19th Century, people with disabilities and inhumane conditions, where they were supposedly housed and educated, were addressed in the literature of Charles Dickens.

Thus attention to the downtrodden conditions of people with disabilities resulted in reforms including the re-evaluation of special schools in Europe. Throughout the mid-half of the 20th century, special schools were not only accepted but also encouraged the students with disabilities.

Deinstitutionalization began in the 1970s following the exposer of the institutions in the US, and it took sometime for the Education for All Handicapped Children's Act of 1974, Individuals with Disabilities Education Act (IDEA) with Disabilities Educational Improvement Act (IDEIA) to enact. School integration was supported as early as the 1970s, and teacher preparation programmes in higher education have carefully taught and instructed graduates on inclusion at the classroom, individual, school, and district levels for decades resulting in dual certification of "regular teachers".

With the amendments to the Individuals with Disabilities Act of 1997, school districts in the United States began to slowly integrate students with moderate and severe special needs into regular school systems. The term 'Special Need Education' (SNE) is now used as a replacement of term 'Special Education'.

5.1 CONCEPT OF SPECIAL EDUCATION

It is the educational programmes and practices designed for students—differently-abled or gifted students—whose mental ability, physical ability, emotional functioning, etc. requires Special Education Needs (SEN)—special teaching approaches, equipment, or care within or outside a regular classroom.

It is classroom or private instruction, involving techniques, exercises, and subject matter designed for students whose learning needs cannot be met by a standard school curriculum.

Special education is specially designed, individualized or group instruction or special services or programmes provided to a student with a disability (SWD) as determined by the Committee on Special Education (CSE).

The Individuals with Disabilities Act (IDEA) defines Special Education as "specially designed instruction, at no cost to the parents, to meet the unique needs of a child with a disability". Education broadly identifies the academic, physical, cognitive and social-emotional instruction offered to children who are faced with one or more disabilities. Some terms that are used in special education are:

Individualized Education Programme

Individualized education programme (IEP) means a written statement, developed, reviewed and revised in accordance with section 2004 of the Regulations of the Commissioner, for purposes of meeting the unique educational needs of a student with a disability.

Least Restrictive Environment

Least restrictive environment (LRE) means that placement of students with disabilities in special classes, separate schools or other removal from the regular educational environment occurs only when the nature or severity of the disability is such that even with the use of supplementary aids and services, education cannot be satisfactorily achieved. The placement of an individual student with a disability in the least restrictive environment shall:

- provide the special education needed by the student;
- provide for education of the student to the maximum extent, appropriate to the needs of the student with other students who do not have disabilities; and
- be as close as possible to the student's home.

Differently Abled

The Constitution of India ensures equality, freedom, justice and dignity of all individuals and implicitly mandates an inclusive society for all including the persons with disabilities. As per the provisions of the persons with Disabilities Act, 1955, seven categories of disabilities have been identified viz., blindness, low vision, leprosy cured, hearing impairment, locomotor disability, mental retardation and mental illness. Persons falling under the above categories with a minimum of 40% disability are eligible for entitlement of all benefits provided by the Government.

Student with a Disability

'A student with a disability as defined in section 4401(1) of Education Law (New York), who has not attained the age of 21 prior to September 1, and who is entitled to attend public schools pursuant to section 3202 of the Education Law and who, because of mental, physical or emotional reasons, has been identified as having a disability and who requires special services and programmes approved by the department.' Some categories of disabilities are:

- Autism
- Emotional disturbance
- Learning disability
- Intellectually challenged
- Multiple disabilities
- Loco motor impairment
- Other health-impairment
- Speech or Hearing impairment
- Traumatic brain injury
- Visual impairment including blindness
- Hyperactive

From the above discussion, we may conclude that Special Education programmes are designed for those students who are mentally, physically, socially and/or emotionally delayed. This aspect of "delay," broadly categorized as a developmental delay, signifies an aspect of the child's overall development (physical, cognitive, scholastic skills), which place them behind to their peers. Due to these special requirements, students' needs cannot be met within the traditional classroom environment. Special

Education programmes and services adapt content, teaching methodology and delivery instruction to meet the appropriate needs of each child. These services are of no cost to the family and are available to such children until they reach 21 years of age.

Special education is a form of instruction which is designed to meet the needs of students with disabilities, so that they can learn the same skills and information as other children in school.

5.2 INCLUSIVE EDUCATION

Inclusiveness education means that schools should accommodate all children regardless of their physical, intellectual, social, emotional, linguistic or other conditions. This should include disabled and gifted children, street and working children, children from remote or nomadic populations, children from linguistic, ethnic or cultural minorities and children from other disadvantaged or marginalized areas or groups (UNESCO, 2003).

Inclusive education means that all students regardless of their ability level are included in regular classes and are supported to learn, contribute and participate in all aspects of the life of the school as equals. In simple words, inclusive *education* means an education system meant for all kinds of learners.

Inclusive education "is a process of strengthening the capacity of the education system to reach out to all learners". "It involves restructuring the culture, policies and practices in schools, so that they can respond to the diversity of student in their locality." For a school to be inclusive, the attitudes of everyone, including administrators, teachers, and other students, are to be positive towards differently abled, socially disadvantaged and marginalized such as the SCs, STs and minorities-students and that allow each student respected and confidant.

About 'Diversity' and 'Inclusive Practice' the term diversity when used to describe people or communities, indicates that a group of people made up of individuals who are different from each other in some way. For example, diversity may relate to differences in culture and/or language

- Gender
- Appearance
- Lifestyle
- Social and economic circumstances
- Family structure
- Abilities, e.g. physical, social, creative, intellectual
- Values and beliefs.

In describing the provision of a service, the term inclusive practice refers to the principle that a service must be responsive to the needs of all users and that diversity will be acknowledged and respected. Inclusive practice means the service will not discriminate against people or treat them unfairly on the basis of these differences, and that negative stereotypes will be challenged.

Inclusive education is about how we develop and design our schools, classrooms, programmes and activities so that all students learn and participate together with inclusive curriculum.

Basic Philosophy behind inclusive education is that those who are among the category of special needs children should be provided education in the normal schools along with normal students. Schools have to fine tune their resources and infrastructure accordingly. Inclusion is an educational approach and philosophy that provides all students with community membership and greater opportunities for academic and social achievement.

5.3 PRINCIPLES OF INCLUSIVE EDUCATION

- Promoting child-friendly learning by removing barriers to learning and participation.
- Increasing learning and participation by developing cultures, policies and practices to include all students.
- Safeguarding the interests of all students.
- Giving access to all students (disabled and ablde) to appropriate education to achieve their potential.
- Promoting a supportive culture of learning that encourages collaboration and problem solving.

Seven Principles for Inclusive Education

The *Seven Principles* for inclusive education can be applied to any classroom or lesson plan to increase equity and decrease exclusion.

1. Teaching All Students

Educators should take several different approaches to teaching the same material so that information becomes more interesting and tangible to a greater number of students.

2. Exploring Multiple Identities

Students who are proud of themselves and excited by the world around them will be more compassionate and understanding towards people; the same is true for educators.

3. Preventing Prejudice

Educators should take a proactive approach to debunking preconceived stereotypes and preventing them from escalating into prejudices and negative biases.

4. Promoting Social Justice

Students are good judges of what is fair, especially when they are affirmatively challenged to consider issues of social justice. Educators should talk to them about issues of social justice and injustice in terms of fair versus unfair, respectful versus disrespectful.

5. Choosing Appropriate Materials

Inclusive classrooms use books and materials that reflect accurate images of diverse people and challenge stereotypes.

6. Teaching and Learning about Cultures and Religions

Educators should create curiosity and expand students' horizon by teaching about others in a positive manner. Students should have the opportunity to learn from their peers as well as other cultures.

7. Adapting and Integrating Lessons Appropriately

Educators should be flexible when using and adapting lessons in our curricula, as well as in prescribed curricula in general. Many of the most teachable moments are unplanned and unscripted.

Guiding Principles of Inclusive Education

- All students have the right to receive a public education in the regular classroom.
- Inclusive education at all levels benefits students with special needs and their peers.
- Each student is unique and needs an individualized approach to education to meet his or her intellectual, physical, social, and emotional and career development goals.
- Parents are valuable contributing partners in the education system and their involvement enhances the effectiveness and accountability of the school system.
- Parents have a responsibility to be involved in their child's

education and schools have the responsibility to encourage parental involvement.
- Students' participation in all aspects of school life is vital to a rich education experience.
- Transitions are more successful for students when formalized student-centered planning occurs.

Benefits of Inclusive Education

All children benefit from inclusive education. It allows them to:

- Develop individual strengths with variety of opportuniy of interactions with peers.
- Work on individual goals while participating in the life of the classroom with other student of their own age.
- Involve their parents in their education and activities of their local schools.
- Children learn a good deal about tolerance and communicate by interacting with each other.
- Foster a school culture of respect and belonging. Inclusive education provides opportunities to learn about and accept individual differences, lessening the impact of harassment and bullying.
- Develop friendships with a wide variety of other children, each with their own individual needs and abilities.
- Positively affect both their school and community to appreciate diversity and inclusion on a broader level.

5.4 GIFTED CHILDREN

Children with Special Need or Exceptional Children

Exceptional children can be defined as those who deviate from what is supposed to be average in social, physical, emotional or mental characteristics to such an extent that they require special guidance services in order to develop their maximum capacity.

Cognitive or Mentally Exceptional

In this group, children who deviate from the average of NPC (Normal Possibility Curve)/NDC to an acceptable limit on both the sides, are included.

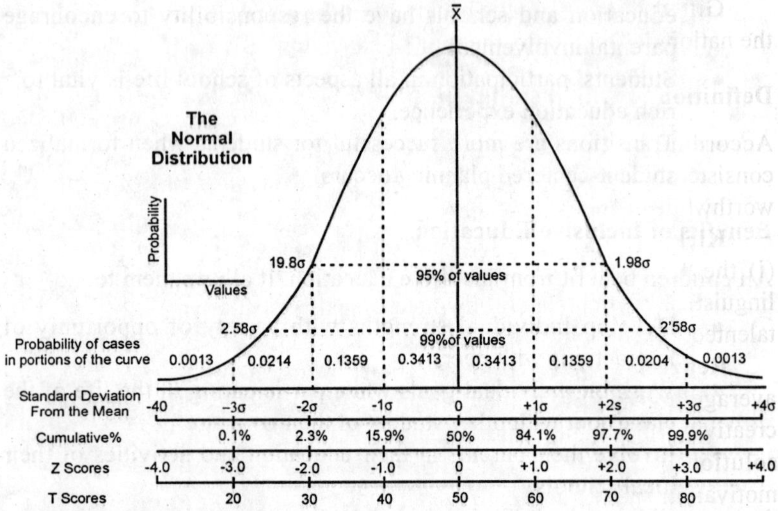

On (+)ve side we have—

- Bright
- Gifted
- Intellectually superior children

On (-)ve side we have—

- Low Achievers
- M.R/MH/Intellectually challenged

IQ – Classification Table

IQ – Range	*Classification*
140+	Gifted
130 -139	Very superior
120-129	Superior
110 - 119	Bright Normal
90 - 109	Average or Normal IQ
80 – 89	Below Average/Slow Learners
70 - 79	Mentally Deficient
50 -69	Mild M.R.(Educable Special School)
35 - 49	Moderate M.R.(Trainable)
20 - 34	Severely M.R.(Socially Subnormal)
Below 20	Profoundly M.R.(Needed Custodial Care)

Source: WHO and NIMH.

Gifted children are the backbone of the nation. The development of the nation depends upon the type of education provided to them.

Definition of Gifted Children

According to **Havighurst**: "The gifted children is one who shows consistently remarkable performance or outstanding behaviour in any worthwhile endeavours."

Kirk's view: "Giftedness is any of the special aptitudes and talents: (i) the academically talented, (ii) the artistically talented, (iii) the linguistically talented, (iv) the mechanically talented, (v) the musically talented, (vi) the physically talented and (vii) the socially talented."

Renzulli's view: Gifted are those who demonstrate – (i) Above average/high ability (including high intelligence), (ii) high level of creativity (the ability to formulate novel ideas and apply them to the solution of problem), (iii) high task commitment (a high level of motivation and the ability to see a project through its completion)."

Factors Contributing to Giftedness

1. The great determining factor of innate mental superiority is heredity.
2. Environment is the factor that determines whether the innate ability will get the opportunity to come to its own or not.

According to Thorndike (1938), high ability or mental superiority is due to –

i. a fairly favourable quality in the genes,
ii. favourable training which such genes create, and
iii. favourable training which parents, friends and society in general provide.

Physical Conditions related to Giftedness:

- Good health (Physical & Mental)
- Nervous Disorder absence
- Mortality Rate less (death rate)
- Special Ability–rich
- Leisure Interests—more
- Personality characteristics
  - Trust worthy

- ➢ Emotionally mature
- ➢ Extrovert
- ➢ Adjustable
- Scholastics Achievement—high

Identifying the Gifted Children

- Intelligence tests/ performance/ mental ability tests
- Achievement tests/ School Accomplishment
- Aptitude Test
- Reports from parents
- Reports from teachers and other professionals
- Reports from peer group
- Age Grade status

Recognizing the Characteristics of Gifted Children

There are three types of characteristics of gifted children:

1. General behavioural,
2. Learning and
3. Creative characteristics.

General Behaviour Characteristics

Gifted children's behaviour differs from that of their age-mates in the following ways:

- Many gifted children learn to read early, with better comprehension. As much as half the gifted and talented population has learned to read before entering school.
- They often read widely, quickly, and intensely and have large vocabularies.
- They commonly learn basic skills better, more quickly, and with less practice.
- They are better able to construct and handle abstractions.
- They often pick up and interpret non-verbal cues and can draw inferences that other children need to have spelled out for them.
- They can work independently at an earlier age and can concentrate for longer periods.
- Their interests are both widely eclectic and intensely focused.

- They often have seemingly boundless energy, which sometimes leads to a mis-diagnosis of hyperactivity.
- They usually respond and relate well to parents, teachers, and other adults. They may prefer the company of older children and adults to that of their peers.
- They like to learn new things; are willing to examine the unusual, and are highly inquisitive.
- They tackle tasks and problems in a well-organized, goal-directed, and efficient manner.
- They exhibit an intrinsic motivation to learn, find out, or explore and are often very persistent. "I'd rather do it myself", is a common attitude in them.

Learning Characteristics

Gifted children are natural learners who often show many of these characteristics:

- They may show keen powers of observation.
- They may read a great deal on their own, preferring books and magazines written for children older than they are.
- They often take great pleasure in intellectual activity.
- They have well-developed powers of abstraction, conceptualization and synthesis.
- They readily see cause-effect relationships.
- They often display a questioning attitude and seek information for its own sake as much as for its usefulness.
- They are often sceptical, critical, and evaluative.
- They often have a large storehouse of information about a variety of topics, which they can recall quickly.
- They quickly perceive similarities, differences, and anomalies.
- They often attack complicated material by separating it into components and analyzing it systematically.

Creative Characteristics

Gifted children's creative abilities often set them apart from their age-mates. These characteristics may take the following forms:

- They are fluent thinkers, able to generate possibilities, consequences, or related ideas.

- They are flexible thinkers, able to use many different alternatives and approaches to problem solving.
- They are original thinkers, seeking new, unusual, or unconventional associations and combinations among items of information.
- They can also see relationships among seemingly unrelated objects, ideas, or facts.
- They are elaborate new steps, ideas, responses.
- They are willing to entertain complexity and seem to thrive on problem solving.
- They are good guessers and can readily construct hypotheses or "what if" questions.
- They often are aware of their own impulsiveness and irrationality, and they show emotional sensitivity.
- They are extremely curious about objects, ideas, situations, or events.
- They often display intellectual playfulness and like to fantasize and imagine.
- They are sensitive to beauty and are attracted to aesthetic values.

Guidance Programme for Gifted

Generally two methods are suggested—

1. Enrichment method
2. Acceleration method

Enrichment Method –

i. Panel Discussion
ii. Project Assignment
iii. Independent study
iv. Use of reference books
v. Pursuit of hobbies and other creative activities.
vi. Special classes

Acceleration Method

i. Double promotion or Grade skipping
ii. Providing enriched courses

iii. Providing for summer school and special workshops
iv. Making provision for advanced level courses while in school
v. Providing for additional subjects while in mainstream course.
vi Admission at earlier stage

Various Schemes for Gifted Children

- Jawahar Navodya Vidyalaya (approx. 350 schools in India), Ministry of Human Resource Development
- Navyoug schools in Delhi, GNCT
- Merit Scholarships Scheme by States and Centre
- National Talent Search Scheme by NCERT, scholarships per year, to study up to Ph.D. level
- National Loan Scholarships (poor families)
- Pratibha Vikas Vidyalayas of Directorate of Education, Delhi

Some Myths about Gifted Children

Gifted Kids are like cream that rises to the top in a classroom: Gifted Children can have hidden learning disabilities that go undiscovered because they can easily compensate for them in the early years. As time goes on, it becomes harder and harder for them to excel, which can lead to behavior problems and depression.

Gifted Kids are so smart that they can do fine with or without special programmes: They may appear to do fine on their own. But without proper challenge they can become bored. As the years go by, they may find it harder, as work does become more challenging, since they never faced challenge before.

Gifted and Talented means the same thing: Not necessarily. There is no rule that states that a child who is capable of scoring ninety percentile on group achievement testing **must** be considered gifted. At the same time, there is no rule that states a child identified as gifted should be achieving high standards in the classroom. This type of stereotyping can do serious and irreversible damage to both groups. Any child can benefit from enrichment. Academically Talented Children can benefit from Honors (Grade Level) Classes. Intellectually Gifted children need a differentiated curriculum and possibly even a different environment.

They need to go through school with their own age mates: While it's true that children need to play and interact socially with other children of their age. They do not need to learn with them, especially in the case of a highly gifted child who may have a chronological age of six and a mental age of 11, who has been reading since the age of two. To put that child in a reading class with other six year olds who are just learning to read is not good for that child.

Giftedness is something to be jealous about: This is perhaps the most damaging myth. More often than not gifted children can feel isolated and misunderstood. They have more adult tastes in music, clothing, reading material and food. These differences to other children can cause them to be shunned and even abused verbally or physically by other children. Experts in the field of gifted education are beginning to address the higher incidences of ADHD and Spelling/Handwriting disabilities in the gifted population is different from those found in the larger normal population.

5.5 LEFT HANDERS

Handedness is individual preference for use of one hand over the other, known as the **dominant hand**.

There are four types of handedness: left-handedness, right-handedness, mixed-handedness, and ambidexterity.

Types

- *Right-handedness* is most common. Right-handed people are more skillful with their right hands when performing tasks. Studies suggest that 87–92 per cent of the world population is right-handed.
- *Left-handedness* is less common than right-handedness. Left-handed people are more skillful with their left hands when performing tasks. Studies suggest that approximately 10 per cent of the world population is left-handed.
- *Cross-dominance or Mixed-handedness* is the change of hand preference between tasks. This is common in the population with about a 30 per cent prevalence.
- *Ambidexterity*: A truly ambidextrous person is able to do any task equally well with either hand , is exceptionally rare, although it can be learned. Those who learn it still tend to favour their originally dominant hand.
- *Ambilevous* or *ambisinister* people demonstrate awkwardness with both hands. Ambisinistrous motor skills or a low level of

dexterity may be the result of a debilitating physical condition, such as dysgraphia (inability to write coherently).

Personality Traits of Left Handed People

Left handed people have always prompted interest. There is science that proves that lefties are actually using their brain a bit differently so they do have some personality traits that are predominant.

Left handed people are typically more creative than right handed people. It may be because in the world where every gadget and tool is made for right handed people. Thus, if for left handed, creativity is less of a trait and more of a necessity. Being adaptable may be something that lefties have had to develop to live peacefully in a right handed world.

Being left handed is actually a symptom of a slightly different brain anatomy.

Abstract Thinkers: Left handed people are well known for being able to look at situations from a deductive reasoning position. While they are historically considered the dreamers, they actually share very logical thinking patterns. They are less irrational than right handed people and can easily divest themselves from the equation when they are trying to solve a problem.

Their independent abstract thinking spills over into their personality and helps them to be perceived as great leaders.

Research has shown that left handed people are more likely to practice inductive logic when solving a problem. This research has also identified that the two top fields for left handed people are technology and the arts. Oddly enough both require the ability to think outside the box to be able to use logic because both are heavy in technical expertise.

Independence: Left handed people are less likely to follow trends. They are typically the creator of trends. They have rebellious personalities which is not necessarily a negative one. The rebellious personality type can be channelled into a positive role and be used to affect necessary change.

Higher Intelligence: Lefties score better in IQ tests that right handed people do under the same conditions.

Socially Powerful: Most lefties are extroverts. They are easy to get along with and are usually socially active. They are energetic personality types that can be impulsive and come across as being free spirited.

Some Famous Left Handers

Narendra Modi

Ratan Tata

Sachin Tendulkar

Amitabh Bachchan

Alexander The Great

Charlie Chaplin

Barack Obama

Bill Gates

Albert Einstien

Social Stigma and Repression of Left-handedness

Many tools and procedures are designed to facilitate use by right-handed people, often without even realizing *difficulties placed on the left-handed. John W. Santrock has written, "For centuries, left-handers have suffered* unfair discrimination in a world designed for right-handers.

McManus noted that, at the time of the beginning of the Industrial Revolution, workers needed to operate complex machines that were almost certainly designed with right-handers in mind. This would have made left-handers more visible and at the same time appear less capable and more clumsy. During this era, children were taught to write with a dip pen. While a right-hander could smoothly drag the pen across paper from left to right, a dip pen could not easily be pushed across by the left hand without digging into the paper and making blots and stains.

Moreover, apart from inconvenience, left-handed people have been considered unlucky or even malicious for their difference by the right-handed majority. In many European languages, including English, the word for the direction "right" also means "correct" or "proper". Throughout history, being left-handed was considered negative. The Latin adjective *sinister* means "left" as well as "unlucky", and this double meaning survives in European derivatives of Latin, including the English word "sinister" (only when referring to the bearer's left of a coat of arms).

There are many negative connotations associated with the phrase "left-handed": clumsy, awkward, unlucky, insincere, sinister, malicious, and so on. A "left-handed" compliment is considered one that is unflattering or dismissive in meaning. The name "Dexter" derives from the Latin for "right", as does the word "dexterity" meaning manual skill. As these are all very old words, they would tend to support theories indicating that the predominance of right-handedness is an extremely old phenomenon.

Black magic is sometimes referred to as the "left-hand path".

Until very recently in Taiwan (and still in Mainland China), left-handed people were strongly encouraged to switch to being right-handed, or at least switch to writing with the right hand. Due to the importance of stroke order, developed for the comfortable use of right-handed people, it is considered more difficult to write legible Chinese characters with the left hand than it is to write Latin letters, though difficulty is subjective and depends on the writer. Because writing when moving one's hand away from its side towards the other side of the body can cause smudging if the outward side of the hand is allowed to drag across the writing, writing in the Latin alphabet might possibly be less feasible with the left hand than the right under certain circumstances. Conversely, right-to-left alphabets, such as the Arabic and Hebrew, are generally considered easier to write with the left hand in general. Depending on the position and inclination of the writing paper, and the writing method, the left-handed writer can write as neatly and efficiently or as messily and slowly as right-handed writers. Usually the left-handed child needs to be taught how to write correctly with the left hand, since discovering a comfortable left-handed writing method on one's own may not be straightforward.

International Left-Handers Day

International Left-Handers Day is held annually every August 13 (Since 1976). As the name suggests, it is meant to promote awareness of the inconvenience faced by left handers in a predominately right handed world. It was founded by the Left-Handers Club in 1992, with the club itself having been founded in 1990. According to the club, International Left-Handers Day is, "an annual event when left-handers everywhere can celebrate their left-handedness and increase public awareness of the advantages and disadvantages of being left-handed."

Advantages of being Left-handed

We often end up complaining about the frustrations of being left-handed, but there are plenty of advantages as well.

1. *Being left handed is an advantage in many sports:* Since most players are right handed, many are unused to dealing with those who are left handed. Take baseball for instance. Southpaws having the advantage of already facing first base when they are at bat, can more easily keep an eye on first base when pitching and can cover a large amount of the field when playing in the outfield by having their glove in their right hand. There are specially designed left-handed baseball gloves available (worn on the right hand, so that you can throw left-handed). Other sports that offer an advantage to lefties are fencing, boxing and tennis.
2. *Lefties have a greater chance of being a genius or having a high IQ:* Researchers aren't sure why, but those who are left handed seem to make up a disproportionately large part of those who are highly intelligent. Some think this genius stems from being forced to use both sides of the brain more often, allowing these individuals to more easily process a large amount of information.
3. *Lefties are better able to multitask:* One of the advantages of being left-handed is that it forces brain to think more quickly. What this means for everyday life is that those who are lefties may find it easier to multi-task and deal with a large, sometimes unorganized stream of information. Researchers found that conversations between the left and right sides of

the brain happen more quickly in left handed people. The more dominant the left handedness is, the better these abilities.

4. *Some left-handed individuals have better memories:* While it isn't true for all who are left handed, data from recent studies suggests that those who come from families of lefties tend to have better memories, though only of the episodic kind. The odd thing about this study, however, is that individuals do not necessarily need to be left-handed themselves to have a better memory. These studies show that traits related to handedness may be passed down separately, though some lefties would prefer to think that their left-handed benefits just rubbed off on their right-handed counterparts.
5. *Generally, lefties are better at playing video games:* Some of the traits that make lefties better thinkers and multitaskers also make them better at playing video games. Research conducted by Dr. Nick Cherbuin shows that lefties are better at handling large amounts of stimuli, making them naturally better at killing zombies, playing virtual tennis or fighting off alien hordes in the virtual world.
6. *Left handed stroke victims recover faster than right handed stroke victims:* While the reasons behind this aren't entirely clear, some believe it's due to left handed people having to strengthen both sides of the brain when navigating a right handed world. Because many lefties are better able to use their non-dominant hand, it is easier for them to recover from a stroke that damages one part of their brain. Of course, recovery for those suffering from a stroke is never easy, no matter which is their dominant hand.

5.6 SLOW LEARNERS

Meaning of Slow Learner

A slow learner is a child of below average intelligence, whose thinking skills have developed significantly more slowly than the normal child of his/her age. This child will go through the same basic developmental stages as other children, but will do so at a significantly slower rate.

Some Characteristics of Slow Learner

1. *Developmental:* Child may have immature language patterns or speech problems

2. *Social*: Poor judgement, immature social behaviour, prefers company of younger children
3. *Personal*: Frustration, aggression, anxiety
4. Academic: Child may show proficiency with particular tasks rather than in subject areas, poor memory, difficulties in understanding several steps in a task
5. *Learning*: Child needs to have new information linked to old, faces difficulties transferring information learned in one situation to other situations.

It is a term that describes a student who has the ability to learn necessary academic skills, but at rate and depth that is below average of same age peers. In order to grasp new concepts, a slow learner needs more time, more repetition, and often more resources from teachers to be successful. Reasoning skills are typically delayed, which make new concepts difficult to learn. A slow learner is a child whose IQ is low enough to cause difficulty in regular classroom. According to psychologists, the IQ score of slow learner lies between 70-80. They learn slower than average students and will need additional help to succeed.

Challenges Faced by a Slow Learner

Most slow learners have difficulty planning long term goals and also completing tasks in a given time frame. This happens because the child gets distracted easily and does not have the internal strategies to complete the task at hand. Due to this they sometimes work very slowly and have difficulty in taking multiple instructions. Reasoning skills are typically delayed, which makes new concepts difficult to understand and they require a lot of support.

Classroom Recommendations for Slow Learner

- Repetition, repetition, repetition. Teacher should repeat the same thing over and over, that helps make a concept more concrete.
- Encourage other activities in which the child can experience success and keep them connected.
- Differentiated Instruction
- Tutoring: This helps fill in gaps in basic skills.
- Teach study skills to help a student become more efficient in studying.

- Teach the most important concepts and leave out some of the less important details.
- Peer tutoring

Tips for Parents and Teachers of Slow Learners

Creating awareness among teachers as well as parents towards this problem is a major step in dealing with the problem.

Tips for Parents

- The child's parents should make a schedule with the child, charting out their daily activities and when they should be performed.
- They should help the child to complete and accomplish his/her scheduled tasks. This will help the child feel empowered.
- Parents should identify the child's interests and activities he/she likes and encourage them to take part in them, whether in school or at home.

Tips for Teachers

- Teachers should encourage the child to take part in activities that they like at school and reward them when it is done well.
- When they are not able to finish the task. They should not be demeaned or insulted, especially in front of the entire class.
- It is essential that teachers understand that encouraging the child is of utmost importance. A slow learner will invariably feel demoralized as he/she will not be able to do as well as their peers, but focusing on the things they are good at is the key to boosting their confidence.
- Maintaining open communication with the child is essential to create a rapport with him/her so that he/she is also open to accepting help from teachers, parents and counsellors.
- Encourage other normal children to deal with the slow learner with some empathy. This is especially important, as very few children will be willing to play or interact with a slow learner, because they might not have the patience to explain the rules and help him/her.

Finally, it is essential that both the parents and teachers do not label the child as a slow learner. Treating them like other normal children, for his/her development, is very important.

5.7 FIRST GENERATION LEARNERS

The first generation learners are those who are attending school for first time in their family or throughout the generation no one has attended the schooling system either formal or informal except the child. They are the first to get opportunity to take education.

Characteristics and Problems of first Generation Learners:

- In their family no one is educated.
- Lack of communication.
- They have some potential to learn.
- No guidance at home pertaining to educational and personal problems solutions.
- They are totally dependent on teachers.
- Lack of motivation.
- Lack of proper learning environment at home.
- Problem of adjustment in school and peer group
- Lack of opportunity to express themselves (hesitation).
- Poor socio-economic status does not allow them to purchase teaching learning material.
- They are neglected in their peer group.
- Occasional absence from the school because child is playing important role in the leaning process in the family.

How to Provide Help to First Generation Learner

- By providing guidance and counselling services to their parents.
- Sympathetic attitude towards them.
- Should give them proper love, affection and respect in the class.
- Special classes for them if their school achievement is low.
- Should use interesting methods of teaching.
- Proper motivation and reinforcement to them on time-to-time.

5.8 UNDER ACHIEVERS

Under Achievers may be categorized as *Backward Children*. The children who perform much below their potentialities.

Gowan (1960) emphasised that an "under-achiever" is one whose academic performance falls below the normative range of his/her potentialities.

Characteristics of Under Achievers

- Their IQ range may be in 90-109 (average).
- They have low self–image.
- Lack of ability to set realistic goals and self-discipline.
- They always blame luck for their bad performance.
- They generally perceive themselves as failure.

Psychological Factors related to Under Achievers

- Lack of interest in study
- Lack of motivation
- Introvert personality factors
- Tension in mind
- Poor study habits
- Adolescence age.

Environmental Causes of Under Achievers

- Poor School environment
- Poor Home environment
- Poor peer group/neighbourhood environment
- Low socio-economic status
- Over parental expectations/ambitions
- Inadequate physical facilities
- Authoritarian atmosphere at home
- Lack of appreciation by teachers as well as parents
- Lack of proper guidance and counselling.

Identification of Under Achievers

- Administering IQ test
- Measuring and analysis of scholastic achievements
- Administering achievement tests.

Guidance Programme for Under Achievers

a) If the home environment is unfavourable, then parents' counselling is necessary.
b) Bad effects of neighbourhood and peer group. This should be checked and parents should be informed.
c) School environment should be designed in such a way that all type of needs of children should meet at a point. For example—
   - Provision of multiple and diversible course and suitable learning experiences in tune with their needs and interests.
   - Provision of extra classes
   - Provision of co-curricular activities
   - Provision for child-centred approach in teaching-learning process.
   - Provision of homework, assignments and other projects. Work should be assigned to child and parents should be informed of that.
   - There should be democratic atmosphere in the class and at home, so that child can express his/her feelings easily and freely.
   - Motivational approach should be adopted while teaching.
   - Provision of trained psychologist and counsellors in the school to deal with psychological needs of the students. If it is not possible, then school teachers should be trained properly to tackle their psychological needs and to deal with them effectively.
   - Individual attention in the class by the teacher.
   - Maintenance of proper cumulative record card.

5.9 CREATIVITY AND ITS DEVELOPMENT

Definition

"Creativity is the power of human mind to create new contents by transforming relations and thereby generating new correlates".

Spearman

"Creative process is any process by which something new is produced – an idea, an object including a new form of arrangement of old elements" A new creation must contribute to the solution of some problem.

—*Wilson R.C. and Guilford J.P.*

"Creativity implies the production of a totally or partially" novel identity". —*R. Stranger and Karwoski T.F.*

"Creativity is the capacity of a person to produce composition, products or ideas which are essentially new or novel and previously unknown to producer". —*Drevdahl*

"It is the process of generating unique products by transformation of existing products". —*Welsch (1980)*

"Creativity implies the production of a totally or partially novel identity". —*Stagner & Korwoski*

From the above definitions, creativity has following characteristics —

i. It should be novel and original
ii. It should be useful
iii. It should be socially acceptable
iv. It should include new combinations of old components.

Nature and Characteristics of Creative Children

According to Torrance, creative children have some unique characteristics. These are–

i. They are curious to know more and more about the problems in hand.
ii. They do not easily accept the traditional solutions of the problems. in hand.
iii. They take independent judgements in crucial matter.
iv. They are independent in thinking.
v. They have strong conviction in their beliefs and values.
vi. They concentrate all the energy on the tasks in hand.

Some other characteristics are:

1. Creativity is universal.
2. Creativity is innate as well as acquired.
3. Creativity produces something new or novel.
4. Creativity is adventurous and open thinking.
5. Creativity is a means of novelty, it is not end in itself.
6. Creativity and intelligence do not necessarily go hand-in- hand.

7. Creativity rests more on divergent thinking than on convergent thinking.
8. Creativity can not be separated from intelligence.
9. Creativity and school achievements (scholastic achievements) are not correlated.

Identification of Creative Children

Creative children can be identified in the following ways –

a. By observing day-to-day behaviour of the child.
b. By studying the cumulative record card maintained by school.
c. By using standardized test of creativity
   Indian Tests—
   - Baker mehndi and test of creative thinking
   - Passy tests of creativity

   Foreign test–
   - Guilford test of creativity
   - Walsh & Kagan test of creativity
   - Torrance test of creative thinking

Stages in Creative Thinking

Graham Walls has suggested 5 steps of creative thinking based upon various researches on different people, and produced five steps of creative thinking:

1. *Preparation:* Thinker prepares and collects data for a new situation.
2. *Incubation:* In this stage, ideas which are interfering with the solution tend to droped out or filtered out. A lot of un-conscious thinking takes place during incubation.
3. *Illumination:* An idea from the solution suddenly comes up in this stage.
4. *Evaluation:* In this stage the thinker tests or checks the solution to see whether it is satisfactory or not.
5. *Revision:* If there is anything wrong in the solution then revise the solution and correct it.

Thinking Involved in Creativity

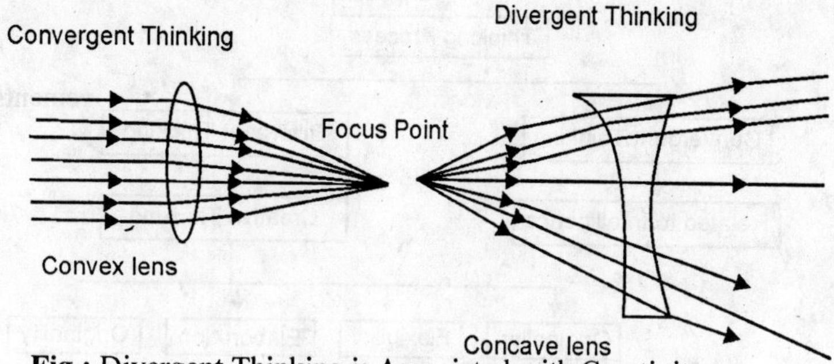

Fig.: Divergent Thinking is Associated with Creativity

Nurturing and Stimulation of Creativity

i. Freedom to respond
ii. Opportunity for ego involvement
iii. Encouraging originality and flexibility
iv. Removal of hesitation and fear
v. Providing appropriate opportunities and atmosphere for creative expression
vi. Developing healthy habits among children
vii. Using the creative resources of community
viii Avoidance of blocks to creative thinking
ix. Proper organisation of the curriculum
x. Reform in the evaluation system
xi. Use of special techniques for fostering creativity
    i. Brainstorming
    ii. Use of teaching models
    iii. Use of gaming techniques
xii. Teaching by examples

Analysis of Thought Process

See Fig. on next page.

Personality and Behaviour Characteristics of a Creative Child:

Cattell (1968), Torrance (1962), Mackinnon (1962) and foster (1971), conducted researches on creative and non–creative persons. On the basis

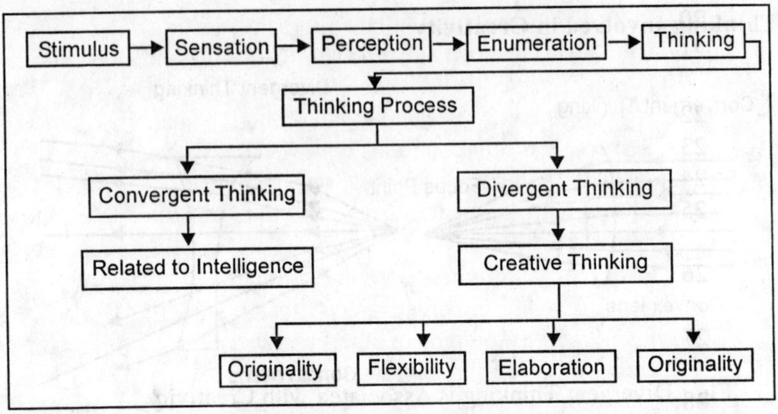

Fig.: Analysis of Thought Process

of their researches and they found the following personality and behaviour characteristics in the creative child:

1. Originality of ideas and expression.
2. Adaptability and a sense of adventure.
3. Good memory and general knowledge.
4. A high degree of awareness, enthusiasm and concentration.
5. An investigative and curious nature.
6. Lack of tolerance for boredom, ambiguity and discomfort.
7. Foresight.
8. The ability to take independent decision.
9. An ambitious nature and interest in vague, even silly ideas.
10. An open mind with preference for complexity, asymmetry and incompletes.
11. A high degree of sensitivity towards problems.
12. Fluency of expression.
13. Flexibility in thoughts, perception and action.
14. Ability to transfer learning or training from one situation to another.
15. A creative imagination.
16. Diversity and divergence of thoughts even in convergent and stereotype situations.
17. Ability to elaborate, to work out the details of an idea or a plan.
18. Absence of fear and even attraction to the unknown, the mysterious and the unexplained.
19. Enthusiasm for novelty of design and even for solution of the problems.

20. Pride in creation (ego satisfaction).
21. Peace with his own self, so that he has more time for creative pursuits.
22. High aesthetic values and good aesthetic judgements.
23. Self respect, self–discipline and a keen sense of justice.
24. Awareness of obligations and responsibilities.
25. Ability to accept tentativeness and to tolerate and integrate the opposite.
26. Pattern of thoughts different from those of less creative, particularly during creative activity.
27. Respect for the opinion of others and acceptance of disagreement and opinions different from one's own.
28. Spontaneity and ease of expressions.
29. Capacity to fantasize and daydream.

5.10 CHILDREN WITH DISABILITY

Impairment

A decrease in strength or value, any abnormality of, partial or complete loss of, or loss of the function of a body part, organ, or system; this may be due directly or secondarily due to pathology or injury and may be either temporary or permanent. Examples include, muscle weakness, pain and loss of joint motion.

Disability

Lack of or restricted ability to perform an activity in the manner or within a range considered normal by the society.

Handicap

A disadvantage for a given individual resulting from a disability that limits or prevents fulfillment of a role considered normal for that individual.

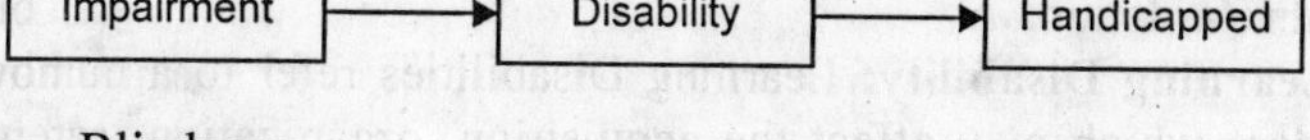

- Blindness
- Low Vision
- Leprosy Cured

- Speech and Hearing Impairment
- Loco motor Challenged
- Mental retardation or Intellectually Challenged
- Mental Illness
- Learning Disability
- Autism
- Crippled or Multiple Disabled

Blindness: Blindness refers to total absence of sight.

Low Vision: Low Vision refers to a condition in which Visual acuity not exceeding 6/60 or 20/200 (Snellen) in the better eye with correcting lenses; or limitation of the field of vision subtending an angle of 20 degree angle or worse.

Leprosy Cured: Leprosy cured person means any person who has been cured of leprosy but is suffering from:

1. Loss of sensation in hands or feet as well as loss of sensation and paresis in the eye and eye-lid but with no manifest deformity;
2. Manifest deformity and paresis; but having sufficient mobility in their hands and feet to enable them to engage in normal activity;
3. Extreme physical deformity as well as advanced age which prevents him from undertaking any gainful occupation, and the expression "leprosy cured" shall be construed accordingly.

Speech and Hearing Impairment: Hearing impairment means loss of sixty decibels or more in the better ear in the conversational range of frequencies; and resultantly speech not develops.

Loco motor Challenged or Disability: Loco motor disability means disability of the bones, joints muscles leading to substantial restriction of the movement of the limbs or any form of cerebral palsy.

Mental retardation / Intellectually Challenged: Mental retardation means a condition of arrested or incomplete development of mind of a person which is specially characterized by sub normality of intelligence.

Mental Illness: Mental illness means any mental disorder other than mental retardation.

Learning Disability: Learning Disabilities refer to a number of disorders which may affect the acquisition, organization, retention, understanding or use of verbal or nonverbal information. These disorders affect learning in individuals who otherwise demonstrate at least average abilities essential for thinking and/or reasoning. As such, learning disabilities are distinct from global intellectual deficiency.

Learning disabilities result from impairments in one or more processes related to perceiving, thinking, remembering or learning. These include, but are not limited to: language processing; phonological processing; visual spatial processing; processing speed; memory and attention; and executive functions (e.g. planning and decision-making).

Learning disabilities range in severity and may interfere with the acquisition and use of one or more of the following:

- oral language (e.g. listening, speaking, understanding);
- reading (e.g. decoding, phonetic knowledge, word recognition, comprehension);
- written language (e.g. spelling and written expression); and
- mathematics (e.g. computation, problem solving).

Autism: Autism is a mental condition, present from early childhood, characterized by great difficulty in communicating and forming relationships with other people and in using language and abstract concepts.

Crippled or Multiple Disabled: A Crippled or Multiple Disabled person is having two or more types of disability at a time in any combinations.

5.11 IMPACT OF IMPAIRMENT ON CHILDREN'S DEVELOPMENT

Impairment affects the various developmental areas of a child such as social, emotional, language, cognitive etc.

We will discuss the impact of impairment on the various areas of development one by one.

Impact of Impairment on Social Development

Social development means the increasing ability to get along well with one self and others. Social development involves the ability to co-operate with others, make friends, adjust with members of various social groups and tolerate the views of others.

Children with impairment face problem in social development. For example, hearing impaired are isolated, without friends and unhappy in school and neighbourhood. For visually impaired, social interactions are more complicated because suitable visual cues are missing and facial expressions are lost. Also speech and hearing impaired children are generally non-commutative due to poor language development and have problem in making friends and adjust with members of groups.

Due to the impairment, persons have low self esteem and self confidence and therefore hesitate to communicate with others. So their social development is negatively impacted.

Impact of Impairment on Language Development

According to Lock, " Language is the ability to communicate with others. It includes every means of communication in which thoughts and feelings are symbolized so as to convey meaning, including such widely differing forms of communication in written, spoken, sign, gestures, arts etc."

Knowledge of the language and its development depends upon the proper functioning of various organs involved in language such as ear, vocal organs, eyes, etc.

The organs involved in language development do not function properly in cases of visually, hearing and speech impaired persons. Much of what is learned by the normal child is learned by imitating others. Also children must be able to hear speech clearly in order to initiate or learn language. If child is impaired (visually, hearing or speech) then he cannot communicate properly with others or understand them. Communication difficulties often lead to social isolation and poor self concept. Also language deficit causes learning problems that result in reduced academic achievement.

Impact of Impairment on Emotional Development

Emotional development is one of the significant aspects of educational growth and development. Almost all the behaviours of human beings are guided in some degree by emotions. They are prime movers of thoughts and conducts. If a person suffers from any type of impairment he/she faces many emotional problems. Generally they are emotionally weak. It may be due to their poor self concept and esteem. Also they feel discriminated among them by some persons.

Impact of Impairment on Cognitive Development

Cognitive development involves the development of thinking skills related to concepts, abstracts and mental representation. If the child is impaired visually, he usually lags behind sighted children by about a year in object permanence i.e. basic understanding that an object exists whether it is seen or not. Also there is generally a substantial delay in the formation of inner representational system that includes independent action. In case of hearing impairment, the cognitive development is also affected due to lack of sense that gives information verbally to brain.

5.12 PREJUDICE AND DISCRIMINATION AGAINST LEARNER WITH SPECIAL NEEDS

It is important to understand the term prejudice, stereotype and discrimination:

Prejudice: A preconceived, irrational and sometimes unconscious thought, belief, attitude, opinion or emotion which is not based on facts. It may be positive or negative. It often involves strong feelings that can be difficult to change.

Stereotype: A standardized mental picture about a group of people that represents prejudiced attitude or uncritical judgment.

Discrimination: When people act on the basis of their prejudices or stereotypes, they are discriminating. It may mean pulling other people down, not allowing them to participate in activities or denying them something they are entitled to by right or law.

Children of special needs face prejudice and discrimination very often.

Prejudice is learned through living in and observing a society where prejudices exist. Children's opinions are influenced by what the people around them think, do and say; it may be media, peer group etc.

If no one explains that prejudice is wrong, a child may grow up thinking that this is the way it is supposed to be and that people who have been discriminated against deserve this treatment. Some people make judgment about a whole group of people without knowing very much about them and they express with name-calling and give negative treatment.

How does One Recognize Discriminatory Behaviour

As parents of children with special needs, they should be alert and vigilant if there is discrimination against them: For example—

- When the parents bring their children to public facilities like park, train, mall, hotel or any other places and see people whispering while seeing them.

- People ask insenstive questions to parents.
- Public or private buildings lack appropriate ramps, access points, other physical support for person with disability.
- Parents in the neighbourhood do not allow their children to play or talk with the children with special needs.
- Friends and relatives begin to ignore or avoid parents and their children.
- Child with special need feel alone in school.
- People generally use slang expressions to refer to the person with disability.

Effect of Discrimination on Children with Special Needs

Children who are suffering from discrimination become negatively impacted. The negative effects of discrimination on special needs children are as follows:

- Find themselves alone and isolated in life, unable to make friends and play with children in neighbourhood.
- Find difficulty in competing for academics.
- Low self concept.
- Feel that they are burden on their parents.
- Find it difficult to get employment.
- Find it difficult to live normal life like others.
- Find it difficult to get admission into school, colleges of their choices.

Role of Parents, Teachers, Community and Neighbourhood

Role of parents, teachers and community in meeting the special needs of children with disabilities are as follows:

Role of Teacher

- Identification of the children with disabilities in the classroom and referring them to an expert for further examination and treatment.
- Accepting the differently-abled children.
- Making proper arrangement of sitting for disabled children so that they feel comfortable and are benefited by the classroom teaching.

- Co-operating with the special educator or resource teacher if they are available in school.
- Creating such environment in which all learners are equally valued.
- Provide proper guidance to the parents for their wards and various special programmes for them and their progress.
- Developing positive attitude between normal children and differently abled children.
- Trusting students with disability and involving them in all activities of the classroom in which they feel comfortable and take interest. The Teacher should organize various co-curricular activities as games, art and craft, etc.
- Assigning the capable children in supporting the disabled with special needs in their study, games, play and in other general activities. Following Co-operative learning among the disabled and normal children.
- Preparation of teaching aids or adaptation of teaching-learning material to help the children with disabilities.
- Provide motivation to students for their work and responses.

Role of Community or Neighbourhood

- Community should hold awareness raising sessions or awareness campaigns for teachers, parents and other members of community regarding children with disabilities and also for normal children. Parents should be aware about the rights of their children.
- The community should assist them with support of equipment and special learning aids, devices and materials, hearing aids, devices and materials, hearing aids, vision aids and wheel chairs.
- The community in collaboration/partnership with NGO's should provide suitable vocational training and job placement opportunities for children and young persons with disabilities.
- Information and consulting centres should be established in the community where children, parents and others can come for advice.
- Provide the appropriate facilities (like ramps, toilets etc.) to these children, persons in various places of community.

Role of Parents/Family

- Early identification of child disabilities and refering to an expert for further examination.
- Parents are the first teachers of their children. They inculcate attitude, skills, beliefs and values in their children. They provide such experiences that schools cannot. Parents often develop extensive activities to support their children's development in area of disability.
- Parents should learn as much as they can about the disability of their children and programmes that support it.
- Parents should change the attitude towards their children with disability like over protection, rejection etc.
- Acceptance of each child as unique and special. Parents should motivate the child by narating success stories of persons with disability.
- Developing partnership with the school and sharing relevant information about the child's education and development.
- Asking for clarification of any aspect of programme meant for the ward.
- Monitoring child's progress and periodically asking for a report. If child is not progressing, It should be discussed with the teacher.
- Co-operating with teachers (special educator) and school.
- Parents should not hesitate or feel shy to talk about their child with disabilities to teachers, family members and other professionals in the field. They should recognize their children's abilities and strength.
- Parents should take an active role in the child's Individual Education Plan.
- Maintaining an ongoing communication with child's teacher.